Genuine
BLACK AND WHITE
MAGIC OF
MARIE LAVEAU

Hoodoo's Earliest Grimoire and Spell-Book

Burning of Candles
Use of Roots and Oils, Powders, and Incenses
Significance of Cards
Horoscopes with Lucky Days and Lucky Numbers
Guide to Spiritualists, Mediums, and Readers

Restored, Revised, and Edited by

CATHERINE YRONWODE

From the Original Writings of

ZORA NEALE HURSTON
ANNE FLEITMAN
LARRY B. WRIGHT
DOROTHY SPENCER
CYRIL ARTHUR PEARSON
HELEN PITKIN SCHERTZ
THE ALLAN COMPANY
FRANZ HARTMANN
ABE PLOUGH
H. F.

Lucky Mojo Library of Occult Classics
Lucky Mojo Curio Company
Forestville, California
2018

Genuine Black and White Magic of Marie Laveau:
Hoodoo's Earliest Grimoire and Spell Book
by catherine yronwode

© 2018 catherine yronwode
LuckyMojo.com/cat

Text:
catherine yronwode
Zora Neale Hurston
Anne Fleitman • Larry B. Wright
Dorothy Spencer • Cyril Arthur Pearson
Helen Pitkin Schertz • The Allan Company
Franz Hartmann • Abe Plough • H. F.

For more information about these authors, see
LuckyMojo.com/blackandwhitemagic.html

Editor:
catherine yronwode

Cover:
Unknown Artist for Abe Plough, Greywolf Townsend

Art:
Unknown artists and typographers, Greywolf Townsend

Typesetting:
catherine yronwode

Production:
nagasiva yronwode

First Printing 2018 / Second Printing 2019

Published by
The Lucky Mojo Curio Company
6632 Covey Road
Forestville, California 95436
LuckyMojo.com

ISBN: 978-0-9997809-2-3

Printed in Canada.

Contents

Dedication

To Marie Laveau, who no doubt rolls over in each of her three graves every time another version of this book rolls off the presses.

Acknowledgements

First and foremost, i would like to acknowledge and to thank all of the contributors who wrote portions of this book over the years, and most especially those who persistently kept it in print, in many variant editions, from 1928 through 2018. Who they are may never be entirely clear, but i credit them as best i know them: Zora Neale Hurston, Anne Fleitman, Bivins Nom de Plume, Larry B. Wright, Dorothy Spencer, Helen Pitkin Schertz, The Allan Company, Franz Hartmann, Sir Cyril Arthur Pearson, Abe Plough, and H. F. (a Fellow of the Universal Brotherhood).

As always, i give thanks beyond words to my darling and beloved husband, nagasiva yronwode, who spent hours transcribing texts, correcting OCR files, creating the List of Supplies, and working out the kinks on this unusual project. Thanks for the coffee, the milk-foam, and the fresh peaches!

My thanks also go out to Grey Townsend for the cover art and interior illustration. Always ready to jump into the game, he has earned the title of "The Pisces Most Likely to Be Voted a Capricorn by Popular Acclaim."

Thanks to my dear partner-in-typography Fred Burke, whose very presence gives me courage, and to Katrink Karpetz and Holly Windsong Greenwood, proof-readers supreme.

Grateful thanks to Carolyn Morrow Long, whose acquaintance i first made in the 1990s and whose admirable research, writing, and generous sharing of rare printed material has shed much light on the path we both have travelled these many years. Thank you, Carolyn, for your generosity.

And last but not least, i want to thank those who kept the wheels turning at my shop, the Lucky Mojo Curio Co., while i was upstairs in my home office, undertaking this unexpectedly intricate adventure in editing. Thank you, Leslie Lowell, Nikki Wilson, Eileen Edler, Heidi Simpson, Yosé Witmus, Margee Stephenson, Nicole Carevich, Jenne Nelson, Angela Marie Horner, Althea Anderson, Ernie Medeiros, Rowena Sparks, Max Jones, and George Ray Brown. I could not have done it without you!

Introduction

With this edition of the earliest known hoodoo grimoire, commonly called *"Black and White Magic of Marie Laveau,"* i have undertaken an enormous task of compilation and rectification. In the years between 1928 and 2008, at least six texts with similar titles were produced by eight different publishers, and although their contents overlapped in part, each variant edition brought something different to the public. Now, with the last of those variants having gone out of print from its publisher, i feel it is time to craft, from all of the variations, one definitively useful text.

Notice that i said "definitively useful," not "definitively complete."

For the 90 years of its popularity to date, *"Black and White Magic of Marie Laveau"* has been a working hoodoo grimoire or spell-book, and i wish to keep it before the public as such. It is not my intention to provide a fully annotated academic compilation of the previous editions.

Of course, Marie Laveau was not the author of this book. However, the presumed first edition, the lost *"Life and Works of Marie Laveau,"* was composed in New Orleans, the city in which she practiced. Her name appears in Zora Neale Hurston's *"Hoodoo in America,"* in Dorene's and Fulton's *"Old and New,"* Marlar's *"Attributed,"* International Imports' *"Revised,"* Indio's *"Original,"* and Lucky Mojo's *"Genuine"* editions. Each spell is framed as a plea to Marie Laveau for aid in attracting luck or overcoming trouble. Hurston called these the "Marie Leveau [sic] routines," but they are more than mere rehearsed performances. Although written in flowery, pseudo-Biblical language, they accurately reflect the emotional urgency with which clients approach conjure doctors to this day.

By 1940, the *"Life and Works of Marie Laveau"* had became the *"Black and White Magic of Marie Laveau,"* and it has retained variations of that title ever since. Why *"Black and White"*? I think that this 19th century term, intended as a figurative distinction between "good" and "bad" magic, caught the eye of 20th century American authors during the era of segregation. For some, it no doubt evoked the Creole culture of Louisiana. However, for Abe Plough, a Jewish chemist in Memphis, Tennessee, it conjured up possibilities of racial equality, and his Black and White cosmetics line, distributed in African-American communities across the nation, was promoted by *"Black and White"* dream books and almanacs, which in turn gave rise to knock-offs like the *"Black and White Dream Dictionary"* by Van Publishing.

As detailed in the Chronological Bibliography, each edition of this book has a different number of spells, pages, or topics. Most contain 30 to 35 spells. The present edition comprises 53 spells; 50 gathered from previous editions, one found in a novel by Helen Pitkin Shertz, and two adapted from pamphlets by The Allen Company. I have rewritten the post-1940 spells to conform to the literary style of the 1931 Hurston edition.

Most editions of *"Black and White Magic"* are undated, but when a body of text is copied and re-typeset, it is quite common to see errors creep in, and these can be used to establish a chronology. In this case, one such indicative error occurs in "The Secret of Prosperity." This spell is not found in the 1930s *"Hoodoo"* corpus, but when it does appear, in the 1940s *"Old and New"* and the 1960s *"Attributed"* editions, it contains the phrase "morality and conscience," a logical pairing of ethical concepts. By the era of the 1980s *"Revised"* edition, however, the phrase has been erroneously typeset as "mortality and conscience" and this senseless error continues into the 1990s *"Original"* edition as well. Like a sub-lethal genetic mutation that adversely marks succeeding generations, the typo "mortality" reminds us that typesetting is more than mere copying. It is an art.

As indicated in Marlar's 1960s *"Attributed"* edition, this book was "Published for the Trade" — that is, it was intended as an aid to professional hoodoo doctors and Spiritual Church mediums, not as a quick-fix for magical dabblers or desperate clients in search of "instant spells." As with all such books, the inner work of preparation and prayer is barely touched on, because those in "the Trade" are expected to be familiar with the supplies and tools of conjure, and any good medium would know how to prepare work for clients who could not follow the instructions as written.

In comparing the various editions, it is clear that the named herbs, minerals, and spiritual supplies prescribed are indicative, not definitive or delimiting. The listed ingredients may seem inconsistent, but only if one overlooks the fact that common names of plants vary by region, suppliers change over time, and proprietary manufacturers offer their own unique titles for similar products. I have retained some older names in the text (i.e. Helping Hand for Lucky Hand), so if you need to make a substitution, consult the List of Supplies starting on page 92, and choose wisely, with due regard for tradition. Do not let the matter of variants and substitutions become a stumbling block, but think of it as an opportunity to refine your historical knowledge and your personal artistry as a spiritual worker.

WHO WROTE THIS BOOK?

By now i hope you are curious about who wrote this book — or rather, who wrote which portions of it.

Alas, i cannot provide definitive answers to this question, but i can share what i know about the many hands who contributed to it, subtracted from it, reconfigured it, and amended it over the years. Of course, as with any research undertaken so long after the fact, there will be gaps and omissions, and mistakes may have been made. This is a work in progress.

MARIE LAVEAU

Marie Laveau (1801-1881) did not write any portion of this book, but some past editions of *"Black and White Magic"* contain fantastic accounts of her life. Zora Neale Hurston's compilation of 1931 gave her a lengthy write-up, but strangely enough, her name was incorrectly spelled as Marie Leveau. Hurston's fabulized biography is too lengthy to include here, but it is online at LuckyMojo.com/hurston-laveau.html — and i also recommend the factual 2007 book *"A New Orleans Voudou Priestess: The Legend and Reality of Marie Laveau"* by Carolyn Morrow Long.

GEORGE A. THOMAS

Carolyn Morrow Long, a fine scholar of hoodoo history, has written that the lost first edition of *"The Life and Works of Marie Laveau"* was probably created as a sales vehicle for New Orleans' Cracker Jack Drug Store, which stocked the supplies required to carry out the spells. The Cracker Jack was founded in 1907 by Dr. George A. Thomas (1874-1940), a New Orleans physician and pharmacist. Stopping short of attributing the text to Thomas, Long does place the vanished *"Life and Works"* in his shop, for sale to the public at the time Zora Neale Hurston was researching hoodoo in the South.

ZORA NEALE HURSTON

Zora Neale Hurston (1891-1960) is best known as a novelist, but early in her career she was a folklorist. She researched rootwork in the South from 1926-1928 and wrote the 98 page article "Hoodoo In America" for *"The Journal of American Folk-Lore"* in 1931. This included 35 of the present spells, and was partially reprised in her 1935 book *"Mules and Men."* I have long suspected that Hurston, not Thomas, was the actual author or inventor of the lost *"Life and Works."*

HENRI GAMACHE (ANNE FLEITMAN)

The new spells in the circa 1940 *"Old and New Black and White Magic"* from Dorene Publishing bear textual signs of having been written by Anne Fleitman (1906-1990), who used the pseudonym Henri Gamache on such 1940s occult shop classics as *"The Master Book of Candle Burning"* and *"The Mystery of the Long-Lost 8th, 9th, and 10th Books of Moses."* Dorene was owned by the Kay (a.k.a. Spitalnick) family. An abridged and wrongly paginated reprint of the *"Old and New"* was published in 1965 by Moe and Mitzi Trugman's Fulton Religious Supply, successors to the Dorene line.

BIVINS, NOM DE PLUME (MRS. JOHN LE BRETON)

"Bivins N. D. P." is the name affixed to the chapter on "Spiritism" that first appeared in Dorene's *"Old and New Black and White Magic"* in 1940. Some bibliographers have taken this to mean that Bivins wrote the entire book, but such is not the case, for Bivins is merely a cover for plagiarism from *"The White-Magic Book"* by Mrs. John Le Breton, published in 1919 by C.A. Pearson in England. I hold that Mrs. Le Breton was a pseudonym of the publisher, Sir Cyril Arthur Pearson. The name Bivins bears the mysterious suffix N.D.P., which stands for "nom de plume" or pen-name.

DR. ELBEE WRIGHT (LARRY B. WRIGHT)

Larry Bernard Wright (1919-1998) operated one of the largest spiritual supply manufactories of the 20th century. The only past edition of *"Black and White Magic"* in which the handy *List of Supplies* appears is his *"Attributed"* edition, published "For the Trade" by Marlar Publishing, circa 1965. Marlar, along with the Tyrad Company and Worldwide Curio House, was a subsidiary of the Wright Co. of Minneapolis, Minnesota, founded in 1960. Wright also wrote and published popular occult spell books under the names Dr. Elb, Elbee Wright, H. U. Lampe, and C. A. Nagle.

ABE PLOUGH

The *Wedding Anniversary Secrets* text in the *"Revised"* and *"Original"* editions is plagiarized from *"The Black and White Almanac, 1922"* published by Abe Plough (1891-1984), a Memphis-based supplier of herbs, perfumes, cosmetics, and medicines to the African-American market. The cover of this present *"Genuine"* edition is fondly adapted from Plough's *"Genuine Black and White Good Luck and Dream Book,"* circa 1925.

FRANZ HARTMANN

Franz Hartmann (1838-1912) was a German medical doctor, and an author on the subjects of Theosophy, occultism, geomancy, and astrology. A short portion of the text was lifted from his book *"Magic White and Black or The Science of Finite and Infinite Life, Containing Practical Knowledge, Instructions, and Hints for All Sincere Students of Magic and Occultism"* published by G. Redway in England in 1886.

PROF. P. R. S. FOLI (SIR CYRIL ARTHUR PEARSON)

The text on card reading in the *"Attributed," "Revised,"* and *"Original"* editions is plagiarized from *"Fortune-Telling by Cards"* by Prof. P. R. S. Foli, published in 1903 by C. Arthur Pearson, Ltd. in England. Foli is a known pseudonym of newspaperman Sir Cyril Arthur Pearson (1866-1921).

MRS. JOHN LE BRETON (SIR CYRIL ARTHUR PEARSON)

"The White-Magic Book" by Mrs. John Le Breton is a 1919 treatise on divination published in England by C. Arthur Pearson, Ltd. Reprinted many times, its most recent publisher is Red Wheel Weiser. From it was plagiarized the *Spiritism* text attributed to Bivins, N. D. P. One hundred years having passed, the identity of Mrs. Le Breton can only be guessed at, but the book's publisher, Sir Cyril Arthur Pearson (1866-1921), was well-known to use pseudonyms (see Prof. P. R. S. Foli, above) and i am convinced that "Mrs. John Le Breton" was none other than Pearson.

H. F. (A FELLOW OF THE UNIVERSAL BROTHERHOOD)

The chapter on the signs of the Zodiac was added by Larry B. Wright during the 1960s, then copied in the Anna Riva edition of the 1980s and the Indio edition of the 2000s. It is an abridged and uncredited sampling from *"Astrology Made Easy or The Influence of the Stars and Planets upon Human Life"* by the pseudonymous "H. F., A Fellow of the Universal Brotherhood," published by the Wehman Bros. of New York in the 1890s. Wehman kept the book in print through 1939, long after the copyright had expired. The full text was then reprinted in 1972 by Health Research of Mokelumne Hill, California, and again in 2002 by Macaw Publishing. I have reluctantly made further abridgements to Wright's extract, due to space constraints, but i am pleased to credit "H. F., A Fellow of the Universal Brotherhood," at long last, as best i can. Further research awaits!

HELEN PITKIN SCHERTZ

Helen Pitkin Schertz (1877-1945) was a New Orleans newspaper journalist, poet, and novelist. In 1926, the academic folklorist Newbell Niles Puckett stated that "although written in the form of fiction ... [her accounts of hoodoo] are scientifically accurate, being an exact reproduction of what she herself has seen or obtained from her servants and absolutely free from imagination." One spell in this compilation is taken from her 1904 novel *"An Angel by Brevet: A Story of Modern New Orleans."*

THE ALLAN COMPANY AND RICHLE INCORPORATED

The Allan Company, a.k.a. Richle Inc., was established in 1974 in Houston, Texas, as a patent and proprietary medicine company, although when Carolyn Morrow Long visited their shop in the late 1990s she found the owners to be typical readers and rootworkers in the Southern tradition. Their *"Guidebook to Black and White Magic,"* published by Richle Press in 1976, was printed in the form of three 16-page pamphlets, containing a total of 21 spells, called "set-ups." I have selected two of these as representative of their style of working and revised them to fit the present format.

ANNA RIVA (DOROTHY SPENCER)

Dorothy Spencer (1922 -2003) is a name little known to rootworkers, because all of her books, as well as her once-highly-respected line of magical oils, came out under the pseudonym Anna Riva. I believe her to be the author of the *"Revised Black and White Magic,"* for her company, International Imports, later published the identical typesetting job as the *"Original Black and White Magic."* When Spencer retired, her formulas and her book titles were bought by Martin Mayer of Indio Products, a.k.a. Cultural Heritage. Eventually Mayer in turn retired, and the new owner of Indio declined to keep *"Original Black and White Magic"* in print, which triggered my long-awaited chance to restore the text.

CATHERINE YRONWODE

With my husband nagasiva, i am the co-owner of the Lucky Mojo Curio Co. of Forestville, California. I have written numerous books on folk magic and edited a long line by other authors. It is my pleasure to restore the occult shop pamphlets of the 20th century, lightly rewriting them when needed. *"Genuine Black and White Magic"* is my fourth such project.

THE WAYS IN WHICH THE SPELLS CHANGED

The rituals included in this book varied quite a bit through the decades. These changes did not seem "random" to me, so i shall recount them here.

• Spells were deleted over the years

Some rites have persisted through all of the editions of this book, but some were deleted early on and never returned — until now.

I don't know that there was a reasoned choice for the deletions, but there may have been an unconscious one. Among the spells that were ousted we find *The Man Whose Lodge Brothers Gainsay Him, The Man Who Cannot Face His Debts,* and *The Lady Who Cannot Face Her Landlord.* Such cuts only removed spells that addressed problems faced by mature adults struggling with issues of poverty, unemployment, and social discrimination. By eliminating these, while retaining prescriptions for love and luck, the impression was given that the book was aimed at an audience of young females. It became, so to speak, a "teen witch" version of itself, and its usefulness to the wider African-American community was reduced.

• Spells were added over the years

In order to replace the spells that were taken away, new spells were sometimes added to later editions. These tended to focus on providing encouraging uplift and social wellness. A good example of such a later "feel good" spell is *The Hard-Working Man Who Wants Luck.*

• New occult topics were added over the years

Early editions do not contain the chapters on card reading, astrology, candle magic, birthday lore, or a list of supplies. These have proven to be of great help to spiritual workers, so i have retained them and edited them by both addition and compression until they fill their pages evenly.

• Consultations that should have been included were not

The newer spells that popped up in later editions did not include the old-school client supplications or pleas that opened the consultations in earlier editions. These petitions function to teach readers and workers how to deal with clients. Without them, the text is just a "spell-book." In the cases where these were missing, i have taken the liberty of adding them.

THE WAYS IN WHICH THE SPIRITUAL SUPPLIES CHANGED

In revising this book, i have been faced with a number of spells in which, over the years, substitutions of ingredients were made. I shall not detail each one, but i would like to note that they follow a certain logic, and to give examples of how, as an editor, i chose to handle this matter.

• Substitution of "products" for botanical ingredients

In later editions, *The Lady Who Lost Her Business* calls for the use of generic "Drawing Powder" (probably intended to be read as "Money Drawing Powder") in place of a much more traditional mixture of "the Powder of Spices of Cinnamon and the Powder of Wonder of the World" (Ginseng Root) that was prescribed in earlier editions. In all such cases, i have restored the earlier text's botanical materials, provided that the original was neither toxic nor an endangered species.

• Substitution of non-toxic for toxic ingredients

I am not the first editor to notice that some of our older hoodoo books and oral histories call for the use of toxic botanical and mineral ingredients, and to edit older material to render it non-lethal to the practitioner. Such editing can be found throughout all modern hoodoo texts. In the spell for *The Lady Who Lost Her Business,* for instance, earlier editions that called for the highly toxic plant Fish Berries *(Anamirta cocculus)* were given a makeover by both Dr. Elbee Wright and Anna Riva, who prescribed generic "product" substitutions. As an herbalist, i consider that kind of replacement a case of throwing the baby out with the bath water, and i have chosen instead to provide a safe botanical and mineral alternative, namely Allspice Berries, in keeping with the spirit of the older editions.

• Substitution of plentiful species for endangered species

The Lady in the Lawsuit calls for the plant Goldthread *(Coptis spp.* in the Ranunculus family) but it is an endangered species. Wright and Riva both substituted the common plant Five Finger Grass *(Potentilla spp.* in the Rose family). However, as an herbalist, i made a different decision. I chose instead to prescribe Goldenseal *(Hydrastis spp.),* because, like Goldthread, it is a member of the Ranunculus family, and because it has the added virtue of having a common name that is similar to the original.

• Substitution of secular goods for religious goods

Catholic religious images of Jesus and Saint Anthony, and the garter of Saint Michæl, specified by Hurston, disappeared in the Wright and Riva editions, replaced by secular products. However, the Jewish additions of Gamache persisted in those editions. I doubt the cuts were made out of dislike for the Catholic Church. Rather, i think they reflected an effort to distribute the book nationally to Black Americans who were predominantly Protestants, but would accept Jewish magic as "Old Testament" work. That is, i think that the spells would be thought to be more "universal" if the effort was made to secularize them. As it happens, only a few of the original spells did include mention of saints, but as far as i am concerned, the loss of these Creole Catholic call-outs diminishes the specificity of this book as a representation of hoodoo as practiced in 1920s New Orleans. Therefore i have restored, and in some cases edited, the names of the saints.

• Substitution of simple procedures for complex ones

In a number of the spell set-ups, a multiple-day series of incense suffumigations and home-altar candle services, or the making of herbal packets to set about the house or carry, were deleted by later authors, and a quick bath or a mild dusting with a simple body powder replaced the more detailed work. These characteristic substitutions of a bath and a body powder for old-fashioned contact magic or altar work undoubtedly made the spells easier for casual users to undertake, but the traditional practice of rootwork was effaced, and the efficacy of the work was probably diminished as well. In these cases, i have restored the original forms of working.

• Combining the old with the new

As noted above, where baths and body powders replaced altar work or the making of packets, i restored the original and fuller rites — but in some instances, it was clear to me that Gamache, Wright, or Riva had made brilliant additions or changes or provided a valuable improvement, so i retained their supplementary ideas alongside Hurston's 1931 text. Taking this a step further, in some cases, i even added a few of my own suggestions. This is, after all, not an academic restoration, but a working grimoire, a scrapbook of spells accumulated through many decades — and i too am one of the authors, compilers, and editors who have, as subtly as possible, formed this text to suit my own ways of working.

Preliminaries

AN ENTIRE PAGE OF DISCLAIMERS

During the era when hoodoo was no longer identified as a "primitive religion," but was still prosecuted as an "inherent fraud," most editions of *"Black and White Magic"* contained legal disclaimers to protect the authors.

NOTE NUMBER ONE

In presenting this revised edition of research into the works of many of assumed authority in the Occult Arts, Black Magic, White Magic, and Talismanic Magic, the aim of the author is to bring out in a comprehensive way this type of cult belief which has been in practice since time immemorial and which still holds sway among a large population in every country of the world. The promotion or undue influence in advocating superstition is entirely disclaimed by the author, and the author, publisher, and distributor also do not assume responsibility for any action on the part of a reader.

NOTE NUMBER TWO

This book is the modern version of the book called *"The Life and Works of Marie Laveau."* It contains basically the same material and advices as the old printing and also includes horoscopes and other interesting information.

NOTE NUMBER THREE

The author claims no original procedures but merely chronicles things that have been done by this peculiar belief, and the purposes for which they have been done, giving no advice and leaving the thinker to think for him or herself as to what to believe or not to believe, whether there is really any basis in fact, or whether Marie Laveau was a great psychologist working by the power of her spirituality to accomplish such things as she has.

In any event, this book will be some addition to the ways and means of other days and may give a little light to the modern psychologists, spiritualists, and other modern beliefs.

Hoping the perusal will interest you and be of some benefit.

SPIRITISM

Divination is the foretelling of future events or the discovery of things secret or obscure by alleged converse with supernatural powers.

Magic is the use of spiritual powers to manifest one's desires.

To the power of mind may be attributed the extraordinary phenomena produced by mediums who profess to be in touch with the spirit world of angels and the dead. The phenomena of Spiritism actually do occur, even when those who are responsible for them are quite possibly unaware of the nature of their own powers. The levitation of tables without contact, for instance, has been proved beyond all doubt by the evidence of men of science whose names have a world-wide renown.

Likewise, on the Malabar Coast, the home of Indian magic, I have seen a magician — one who practiced the "pretended" art of magic — stretch himself upon a cot brought out from the servants' quarters, and in broad daylight, by sheer mind-force, raise that cot four to six inches from the ground, so that a lath or stick could be passed freely under the legs of it. That was claimed to be magic.

The power of your mind is as real and actual a force as the power of your hand. That which your mind pictures clearly, and your will demands strongly and untiringly, you can draw to you and make your own, sooner or later. No argument is necessary to convince you of the accuracy of this statement, for you can see it working out continually and exactly around you as you go through life.

Rely upon yourself and learn to use your judgement in every detail of your daily life. You have free will and freedom of choice, and if you do not exercise them, the responsibility is yours — and it is one which cannot be evaded. Try to realize the power of your mind. Realize your consciousness, and begin to use it firmly, without a minute's delay. Then choose wisely, concentrating your mind steadily and strongly upon what you have chosen until you have made it your own.

Be very sure that what you desire will be for your benefit — because if you are sincere and strong and persistent in using this great natural force of yours, you will most certainly draw to yourself exactly what you have imagined and that which you have resolved to acquire.

Concentrate your mind-power steadily and strongly upon your desire. Demand, and you will receive.

BLACK AND WHITE MAGIC

The black magician does not obey his own selfish emotions, but controls them and creates emotions in others which they cannot resist, and in this way he accomplishes his purpose. He hates whom he chooses to hate, and his will, if directed against the person he hates, is freighted with evil. His touch may bring disease, and his evil eye may be poison to persons who, having very little will power of their own, cannot resist its influence.

The white magician strengthens and expands his will-power by bringing it into harmony with the universal will. The first manifestation of his will is a universal love for humanity, and each act by which he expresses his love strengthens his will. To unite one's will with the universal will does not mean a merely passive contemplation and perception of spiritual truths, but an active penetration into the process of evolution, and a real cooperation with the beneficial powers, the master-builders of the sidereal universe. He has a strong determination to accomplish whatever is in his power for the good of humanity, and expresses that determination through action. According to the unselfishness and power of such a person, his individual influence may extend over a family, a village, a town, a country, or over the whole Earth.

THE LIFE AND WORKS OF MARIE LAVEAU

In writing this book, it is the aim of the author to bring together all of the history and activities of Marie Laveau, who for a long number of years was known as the Hoodoo Queen of New Orleans and whose fame spread all over the South and then penetrated the North of these United States of America. She was known, feared, and loved by both whites and coloured in her home city, and was called on for advice by people in all walks of life.

Many believed in her and her peculiar religious activities and many scoffed and laughed at her, but she was a power among those who swore by her and practiced her rites and ceremonies, and who, endeavouring to influence the course of events to their immediate benefit, brought their woes, their troubles, and their hopes of happiness to her for solution.

It is authentic history that Marie Laveau at one time was consulted by the Queen of England on a very important matter and after successfully accomplishing the orders of the Queen, she was made a present of a very valuable and unique shawl besides the gift of a large sum of money.

Twelve "Black and White" books, from 1886 to 2001, which either form a part of the present text or share similar titles and imagery.

Preparing for the Work

1. ADVICE TO SPIRITUALISTS AND MEDIUMS

It is generally admitted, and deplored, that many of the best mediums are ill-educated, and sometimes quite illiterate. It may indeed seem strange that departed spirits and angelic beings should deliberately elect to manifest themselves through unschooled vehicles, but it is not at all strange that such people should be capable of exerting their mind-forces to an extraordinary degree, for, having discovered their natural powers, they may concentrate upon their spiritual development unhampered by the influences of a skeptical education. It is also a fact that among highly-educated people, mind-force and spiritual gifts are sometimes impotent through non-use.

Until now, no text-book has been at the disposal of the vast and ever-increasing numbers of those who are eager to study the science of mind, and to unleash their psychic forces through the tremendous power of natural magic. It is the author's hope that this book will serve you well.

My friends, I know you desire to help and to comfort those who come before you with tears in their eyes, painful hearts, distress that mounts from day to day, and no one to turn to but you — but sometimes you are also burdened with your own troubles in addition to the unfortunate afflictions of others. It is not an easy path. It is absolutely necessary that you be in complete control of all your faculties. If you aim to be of service, you must first be spiritually strong yourself, and your strength must be matched by your compassion, in order that you may truly see and attend to the needs of those who seek you out. To help yourself, and to acquire the power to help others, follow these instructions:

On arising in the morning, the first thing to do is to anoint your head with Power Oil, light two small White Candles, pure and blessed with Holy Oil, and meditate or read from Scripture for fifteen minutes.

In your main room or consultation room a White Vigil Candle should always be burning. Be sure it too is blessed with Holy Oil.

Dress your premises with Peace Water at least once a week and in your bath water pour five drops of Master Key Oil once a week.

Sprinkle Jinks Removing Salt on the outside of the building.

Strength will be yours. So Be It.

2. HOW TO SPIRITUALLY DRESS HOMES AND CHURCHES

When you first arrange your rooms, office, shop, or church for spiritual work, you should dedicate the premises. This is one way to do so.

Place on the floor of each room a saucer almost filled with water and in each saucer pour ten drops of Oil of Rosemary and let the saucers remain in place. In each room light also one devotional White Candle and let these remain lighted until they burn out by themselves.

Pour a spoonful of War Water into a basin or pail, add two quarts of hot water, and mix well. Pour this at the four corners of the property, outside.

Then you will pour a spoonful of Peace Water into the bucket or pail, add two quarts of hot water, and mix well. With your hand, you will sprinkle of this mixture in every corner in every room. While doing this you will murmur in a low voice these words:

Ezekiel, Isrælis. May the blessings of God enter here. Amen.

After every room has been sprinkled, you will use the remaining water in the pail or basin and with it you shall make a cross outdoors at the rear of your house, business place, or church. If the place to be dressed is upstairs, you shall throw this water out through the rear window.

This done, you shall light John the Conqueror Incense in an incense burner or small saucer and carry it through every room to be dressed.

Returning to the room from which you started, there you shall kneel in front of the first burning devotional candle and repeat the following prayer.

Almighty God, we beseech thee mercifully to incline thine ears to us who have made our prayers and supplications unto thee; and grant that those things which we have faithfully asked, according to thy will, may effectually be obtained to the relief of our necessity, and to the setting forth of thy glory.

Rise from there and sprinkle Master Key Powder in every corner of every room. After this read the 91st Psalm. When you have finished reading this Psalm, you will gather all of the dishes that contain the Oil of Rosemary and water, and pour them into a bottle to be used by sprinkling a few drops of it in the front part of your house daily until it is all consumed.

After this, kneel again before the first devotional candle and read the 21st Psalm. Be very careful to let the candles burn out before moving them away. When you have done all of these things, my dear child, only divine blessing must be expected in your place of work. May God be with you.

Attracting Luck

3. HELP FOR ONE WHO NEVER HAD SPIRITUAL HELP

O good mother, I come to you with tears in my eyes and a heart as heavy as steel. I am filled with regret for the many years I wasted because of my own ignorance. All around me others have reaped the goodness that life has had to offer, while I had misery and sorrow. Dear mother, I had no one to guide or advise me. I beg of you to help me overcome the years that I have neglected my spiritual life. Humbly, I beg you to lift me from my knees and lead me to a path of spiritual growth and everlasting hope.

My dear child, of all the pleas that come to my ears, yours touches me most deeply. How you must have suffered, groping in the darkness for spiritual help. Now happiness is within your grasp, for I will help you build your mind, body, and home to a higher level. And as you do these things, do not forget the unhappy people who still need a helping hand. For each time we help another we advance toward our own happiness.

You will put ten drops of the Oil No. 20 in your bath at least once a week. Once a month you will cover your body with the Oil of Saint Cyprian and leave it on for one half hour and then take a hot bath with the Oil No. 20. This is best done just before retiring. While in the bath, close your eyes and say the Lord's Prayer. When you have dried, dust yourself with Uncrossing Powder. You will have a sound, restful sleep and bring peace to your mind.

Next, wrap and tie in Red Flannel a Lodestone, a Mojo Wish Bean, and a Lucky Hand Root. Anoint this with Master Oil every Friday, and carry it with you wherever you go. And in the morning use Master Oil as a perfume, saying, *"Dear Lord, please help me."* This puts your body in good shape.

Then to get your home in good order, you will clean it thoroughly, with Van Van Floor Wash in the scrub water. Sprinkle Peace Water in each corner, including cupboards. Sprinkle Jinks Removing Salt outside your front and back doors. Have one small White Candle burning as you do this, and whenever you walk by it, remember to thank the Lord for your blessings.

My dear child, these things you will do to start yourself upward to spiritual heights you did not believe possible. Then you will be in a position to work on any condition that you desire. God bless you. So Be It.

4. A HAND FOR THE MAN OR WOMAN IN BAD LUCK

O my dear mother. your child comes to you with tears in the eyes and a downcast look in the face, for I have lost all that I possessed in this world. My hopes are vanishing and with no one to turn to but you, I therefore implore your help.

Restore to me the smile and happiness that once were mine. I would give part of my life for some of the luck that I used to possess.

O mother, will you hear my prayer and help me?

My poor child, I have listened to your words of sorrow and gladly will I give my help that you may be lucky and happy again.

You will make a small bag of Red Flannel. In it you will place a piece of the Lodestone and a piece of the John the Conqueror Root and one pair of the Adam and Eve Root (or a pair of Balm of Gilead Buds) and a piece of the Root called Devil's Shoe String. Having all of these things in the bag, sew or bind it tight that none of it may come out. This done, hold it in your left hand and with the right hand sprinkle on it five drops of the Holy Oil and at the same time read Psalms 23 of the good book called the Bible.

Place this bag in your pocket or pin it close to your skin and let it remain there, allowing no one to touch it. This bag should be anointed with the Power Oil every seven days, on the fifth day of every week, which is Friday. And at that time you will burn in your house the Lucky John the Conqueror Incense, mixed with Good Luck Mystic Incense, as you recite the following prayer:

O Lord God Almighty, be Thou favourable unto us, though unworthy to lift our eyes to Heaven by reason of the multitude of our offences! O God all-merciful, Who willest not the death of a sinner, but rather his true conversion, bestow Thy grace on us! O Lord, O God, full of compassion, aid us in this hour and grant us our desire that Thy name may be blessed forever. Amen.

You will use every day on your raiment and handkerchief the perfume of Astrology that is known as your Lucky Month or Zodiac Perfume, selected according to the Star Sign under which you were born. To this you may add the Oil of the Planet that rules your Sign, and if you would be most lucky, attend to the lucky days and colours of your sign as well.

After doing all this, my child, go forth and do all that is clean and good and have no fear but that you will receive your desired luck. So Be It.

5. THE MAN WHOSE GAMBLING LUCK WAS CROSSED

O wise mother, my luck in games of chance has fallen away, and it is my belief that I have been crossed by another player, for those from whom I once won many shekels now win with regularity, while I lose equally often, and go home empty-handed. Please tell me, kind mother, how I may restore the luck that was stolen from me, protect myself while at play, and once more win and prosper.

My child, if you know that other players in the game are using some subtle art to cross you up, to interfere with your winning, or to bring you bad luck, you will overcome them by putting Uncrossing Bath Crystals and a pinch of Saltpeter in your bath, and while the water is running, pray Psalms 91. And after the bath, before you dress, anoint the palms of both your hands and the soles of both your feet with Protection Oil.

Thus cleaned, you shall write your name nine times on the back of two copies of the 14th seal of *"The Sixth and Seventh Books of Moses."* For as it says: *The Spirits of the Fifth Table of Saturn will serve in everything according to your wish; their Table will bring you good luck in play.*

You shall place one seal in your wallet to carry with you, but the other seal you shall set beneath an anointed gambling candle, such as the Lucky Number, Lady Luck, Lucky Mojo, or Lucky 13, according to your favour.

To one side of this lucky candle, set your Zodiac Sign Candle and to the other side, set a Protection Candle. Let all three candles burn straight through, night and day, but each morning exchange the two seals of Moses. Carry the one that was under the lucky candle, and place the one that you were carrying under the candle. Exchange them daily until the candle is consumed. Burn Fast Luck Incense daily.

When all three of the candles have finished, place one of the seals in your hat and the other in one of your shoes.

Prepare a lucky mojo hand by sewing a John the Conqueror Root, a Master Root, and a Wonder of the World Root tightly in Chamois skin, and anointing the bag with Master Oil. After it is sealed you will dress it with the oil and let no one touch it. Then take of the Master Oil and place a small amount of this oil on your hands, rubbing them together rapidly until they become warm, and when they are fully heated, make your wish.

Carry the lucky mojo with you at play. If you do these things, your luck shall return and you shall be protected against interference. So Be It.

6. THE LUCKY HAND

O good mother, I come to you to lay at your feet my most deep trouble. It seems that everything that I try to do goes against me. I can get no encouragement from the women and men with whom I speak. When I see a game of chance and put my gold into it, lo, my money diminishes. When I see good merchandise which I can easily sell at a profit, lo, it proves to have no value. When I seek employment, lo, the men who hire turn their heads and will not hear me. So it is, one failure after another, one disappointment after another. I am on my knees before you with a very poor heart, for my spirit is broken and I know not what to do. Will you, good mother, also turn me away and leave me in despair? I pray you that you will call upon the good spirits to help me and take me as your own.

My son, rise up and take heart, for those with willing hands shall not fail, even if evil spirits have conspired against them. I will lend my help to make you strong again. To accomplish this, you will take a whole Nutmeg of the Indies, a small live Lodestone covered with Magnetic Sand, the Root of High John the Conqueror, the Root of Wonder of the World, the Wish Beans, the Cat's Eye, and the resins of Frankincense and Myrrh. And as you pour each thing into a Red Flannel Bag you will say the following prayer:

O good Lord, make me stout of heart.
O good Lord, let my sight penetrate the innermost things.
O good Lord, give me power to speak.
O good Lord, let my words be hearkened to.
O good Lord, drive the evil spirits from me.
O good Lord, give me success.
O good Lord, let me hold all of these things in this bag.
O good Lord, let them never leave me.

And after saying the last prayer of the last thing as you put it in the bag, then sew it up tightly and wear it so that it will never leave you and no one will touch it. And when you wish the good spirits to help you, you will mix the Master Key Oil and the Fast Luck Oil together and put a little of them on the bag. Lo, my good son, this is the secret of the lucky bag. Keep it next to your body that you may feel it in the morning when you first wake up and look upon the Sun, and it will give you power and confidence in yourself and you can go forth without fear. Then all things must come to you, and you shall not know any such word as "failure." So Be It.

7. THE GAMBLING HAND OF THE GODDESS OF CHANCE

Great Goddess of Chance, I would ask your favour. When I go to the race course, the horse does not heed me or make efforts that I may be victor. And the driver does not lash his steed that I may come in first line, but instead lags behind that I may lose my gold and silver.

When I set me down among the select men and play the game of cards, you do not put into my hand the high cards which will undo my opponents; but instead you put into my hand the low cards which will be my undoing.

When I pray to you with the dice in my hand, you do not smile on me, neither do you guide them that they may show a smiling face to me; but instead you guide them that they may turn to the help of other players and I go home with my pockets empty and my heart heavy.

I am your steadfast worshipper and would fain win your favour so that my horse will come to the victory line the first, and so that the high cards shall burn to get in my hand, and so that the dice shall be friendly to me.

Tell me, what can I do to win your approving smile, that I may have in my purse bright gold and jingling silver?

My son, you have asked a great favour of me, but you have not burned any incense at my altar and you have not made any offering to my spirit. For I look only on those who are my steadfast worshippers. Those who come for a day, I know them not, neither do I smile on them. But those who worship, I smile on them, and those of good spirit, I love them.

So if you wish to curry my favour, you will put into a small bag made of Chamois the following holy articles: the Grains of Paradise, the Root called John the Conqueror, the crushed Magnetic Lodestone, the Lucky Stone, and the Tooth of the Shark. These you will close together tightly, and on the day you care to win, you will put on this bag Extract of Has No Hanna and keep it in your left pocket and let nothing touch it except the money you will wager on the games, so that it will multiply and grow.

And on your hands when you are playing, you will put the Essence of the Three Knaves and a King. Pour of this essence in the palm of your hands and rub it dry. And in your house you will burn the Incenses of Mercury and of Good Luck so that you will quickly get your wishes, and so the cards, the dice, and the horses will break in your favour and do as you wish.

Fail not to worship me and love me, for the day you cease to do so will be your loss. Do this and you will enjoy good luck and happiness. So Be It.

8. THE BEST GAMBLING HAND (CALLED THE TOBY)

O good mother, I come to you with a strange request. Unlike many others who seek you out, I have no tears in my eyes and my hands are not empty. I lack not for friendship, nor for love. I am valued at my place of employment and I earn both respect and a fair wage there.

Dear mother, unlike those whom I see huddled before you, my wish is only that, on my days of leisure, I may go forth to play at games of chance, and win. Perhaps this is but a trivial request, for my livelihood does not depend upon my winnings, but I come to you, of all the wise ones, because in my travels I have heard of a powerful hand, which is called the Toby, and I wish to know its secret, to possess it, and to use it to my benefit.

O good mother, if you grant me this favour, I will not abuse the knowledge, and will always contribute a portion of my winnings to the poor.

My dear son, you have asked of me a secret known to but a few. I shall impart this knowledge to you, if you truly use it wisely, and keep your faithful promise to give a portion of your winnings to the poor.

Now, as to this charm, it is called the Toby, but do not hastily undertake its manufacture, for it is not safe to touch, and instead of much money, you may reap much sickness and sorrow by its use. This I shall ameliorate, by showing you a better way to make and have it.

The secret is to take the Nutmeg of India, and in it to drill a hole in which you pour the pure, liquid, metallic Mercury called Quicksilver and seal it with pure wax. This is the danger of the Toby, for Mercury is a deadly poison, and I implore you to abstain from its use. I would have you instead saw the Nutmeg in half, and insert between the halves a silver Mercury Dime, and glue the pieces together with the coin between the halves.

Next, sew a piece of Chamois leather into a small bag. Into this you will put a small but highly magnetic Lodestone, a small John the Conqueror Root, some Devil's Shoe String, and a pinch of Five Finger Grass. You will add to these the two Lucky Stones of the Crocus Fish. On top of these you will place the prepared Nutmeg of India.

This done, you will sew the bag all the way around so that none of these articles may fall out. And on the outside of this bag you shall sprinkle three drops of Jockey Club or Hoyt's Cologne every week. Keep this bag on your person at all times, allow no one to touch it, and give to the poor. So Be It.

9. THE MAN WHO WANTS TO FIND BURIED TREASURE

O mother, I come to you with a peculiar request. Through local talk, and through dreams, and through examination by means of a rod, I have come to believe that in a certain farmer's field, a treasure once was buried. The farmer is long dead and the field is fallow. I wish to find this treasure, and to do so without arousing the wrath of the dead or the enmity of evil spirits. Kind mother, guide me in this undertaking, if you please.

My son, when you first go on the field of treasure, you will walk around it in a square and on the North corner you will plant a piece of the Wonder of the World Root, and on the East corner you will plant a piece of the Wonder of the World Root, and on the South corner you will plant a piece of the Wonder of the World Root, and on the West corner you will plant a piece of the Wonder of the World Root, so that at all points of the compass you will ward off the work of the evil spirits.

And in your right hand pocket you will carry the Infernal Stone, called Lapis Infernalis or Lunar Caustic, which comes from the bowels of the Earth. This you will keep bottled and wrapped up securely, but touch it not, and you must carry it so that no other human hands can touch it. Then, spirit-led to the place where you will dig, there on the spot you will put a seal called the Highest and Truest Seal of Fortune of Moses of *"The Sixth and Seventh Books of Moses"* made in parchment paper and traced with Dragon's Blood Ink. This you will put on the ground. And on your hands you will rub the Spirit Oil made from pure Chinese Oil and Oil of Cedar of Lebanon. This you will rub on your hands before you touch the place to begin digging.

And after you have put down your seal and rubbed your hands, no word shall be spoken that will call the spirits or disturb them in their meditation, for as you have placated them and made them quiet, so must you keep them, that you will have no further trouble with them. And when you find the box or chest wherein there is the treasure, you must silently lift it out and silently exchange it for the Lapis Infernalis, for even when you have it in your hands, until you leave the field, with one word the gold and silver may be turned to dross and become of no value, and all your work come to naught.

So, my son, go you and do all these things that you may become proficient in your undertaking, and that you may find that which you seek, so that your days may be full of joy and that your table will groan under the good things which you have. So Be It.

10. THE HARD-WORKING MAN WHO WANTS LUCK

O dear mother, I come to you to gain something which I, alas, have never had, and that is the spirit of luck. I am well-rewarded for the work I do and have a sweetheart whom I hope to make my wife. But all my gain has only come through diligence and labour. I, alone of all my friends, have never had any luck. When they tell me of their good fortune, I am left to hang my head. I have never won at games nor at the race track, I have never found a coin in the street, no one has rewarded me for returning lost valuables, and no special favours have been bestowed upon me by aged relatives or kindly employers. Good mother, please show me the truth about luck. Is it something I may gain, or was I simply born without it?

Dear friend, your future success may yet be made by that invisible force and element known as luck. Almost every person who has become successful and famous will tell you that they owe much of their great success in life to luck. Your turn may come at any time.

Chance is all about us. The world is filled with chances which, if recognized and acted upon, mean opportunity and success. There is plenty of good luck in this old world of ours, and the supply is inexhaustible. If we think of this we may be surprised to see how easily the luck can go around.

Julius Rosenwald, who began his business career as a church organ pumper at five cents an hour and rose to be the President of Sears Roebuck, attributed the great wealth that he amassed, estimated at 300 million dollars, to pure luck. But in his case, it seems, luck favoured his goodness, for he used his luck, in collaboration with his friend Booker T. Washington, to build 5,000 schools, shops, and teachers' homes in the South, as well as funding the Museum of Science and Industry and low-income housing in Chicago for migrants who sought a better life in the North. Luck found him, and he gave his winnings to benefit others.

Therefore, I will teach you a simple way to find luck. Write the words, *"Health and Wealth for Us All"* on a one dollar bill, dust it with Good Luck Powder, and place it in an envelope. As you have money to spare, add more dollars, each one marked and dusted. Choose wisely an institution that helps the poor. Make your wish, pray for luck, and give, and promise that with luck your next donation will be larger. Join hands with others of like mind, and your philanthropy will be magnified and blessed. May luck follow your goodness and may your goodness be well-rewarded. So Be It.

Attracting Success

11. THE MAN WHO WISHES TO GET A JOB

O dear mother, I come to you with a supplication which I wish you will grant me, for I am at a loss and have no one to whom I can turn for help. Whenever I think that I am doing well in my employment, the evil spirits that surround me interfere with my progress and I find myself without a job. In due time, a new job presents itself, and I am again hired, but in short order, the work ends, the shop closes, or others are promoted but I am laid off without cause. Then I must needs deplete my savings or live off the mercy of my friends as I search for a new position. I have been out of work now many weeks, with no end in sight. I beg of you, dear mother, help me in my hour of need and I will be grateful to you all the days of my life.

My good child, I will hesitate not to tell you how much I sympathize with you in your dark hours, but do not give up hope, for the Almighty watches over you twenty-four hours a day and He will not overburden you more than your frail body can stand. It is the strong in spirit who finally attain the good wishes and the blessings of God.

You shall take of the Crown of Success Oil and with it you will anoint your head every night at nine o'clock for nine nights and you will burn in the house the Incense of the Lucky Hand mixed with the Incense of High John the Conqueror. And in your pocket or close to your skin in a Chamois skin bag you will carry the Lucky Hand Root and the two Lucky Stones, along with a coin of any kind that was either given to you or which you found perchance on the streets. These things should not be seen by anyone except yourself and the work should be done in complete secrecy in order to control the spirits, that they will not divide their attention.

This done, my child, go forth and make the necessary application for your job, carrying with you the good recommendation of your former employer.

And when you go for an interview, have in your pocket small pieces of Gravel Root mingled with Salt. And in your shoe place the name of the one whose charge it is to hire the workers. Do not stop on your first attempt, but keep on, and the good spirits will help you most of the way.

Stop worrying, my dear child, bring a good smile onto your face, and your desires will come to pass. So Be It.

12. THE MAN WHO WANTS TO HOLD HIS JOB

O gracious mother, I come to you with a clean heart and a clean desire, for the protection that I know only you can give me.

At times my employer looks upon me with scorn and disdain, and at other times he showers me with kindness and favours. I have asked for help from good spirits, but I feel that there are also evil spirits working against me, and this job, which I would like to keep, is slipping away from under me.

My nerves are frayed, my hope is fading, and fear is gradually taking possession of my soul and consuming my vitality. I do not know whether my steps lead me forward or backward. Now, dear mother, I beg you to help me keep my position, around which I have built my hopes.

My dear child, as you have well stated in your faithful request, there are both good and evil spirits, and they are working for you and against you.

You have neglected to do the things which you should have done in harmony with the good spirits to drive off the evil ones, but I will help you to eliminate the spirit of gloom that constantly hovers over your head, leaving you in an uncertain state of mind regarding your employment.

You will take the Angelica Root and the Grains of Paradise and you will place them in a small bag made of the skin of the Chamois. This bag you will carry touching your own skin, and every week you shall anoint it with five drops of the Fast Luck Oil.

And every day you shall pour into your bath water three drops of the Oil of Rosemary for the purpose of cleansing your body.

And in your hair rub three drops of the Oil of Crown of Success so that a fresh sweet scent will remain on you.

You shall never let frowns appear on your face at your job, for they tend to draw the spirits of evil, making it difficult for good spirits to assist you.

At bed time each night you will repeat the following prayer:

O great and living God, who hast created man to enjoy felicity in this life, and who has adapted all things for his necessity, be favourable to this, my prayer: Permit not evil spirits to afflict my body or my soul, but grant me, O Great God, the power to dispose of them through your help and to call upon angelic and good spirits for my aid and assistance, and I will forever remain thy faithful and obedient servant. Amen.

And in your right shoe you will wear a copy of Psalms 91, to remove all evil spirits and to draw in the help of good ones at your work. So Be It.

13. THE MAN WHO WISHES TO OBTAIN A PROMOTION

O dear mother, I come unto you to ask for your help. My mind and my spirit have been burdened to the breaking point. I have many gifts, and many skills, but I have not yet found my heart's desire, which is success in my chosen field. When promotions are given, I am not offered one. When extra work is assigned to the employees, I am overlooked. I am at my job every day, but my diligence is not rewarded.

I beg of thee, O dear mother, turn not deaf ears to my supplications, but teach me your ways that I may be successful in those things which I desire, within the bounds of my skills and reason.

My dear child, I understand your tribulations and your trials. Your gifts and skills are greater than your rewards, for bad luck and ill fortune have prevented the achievement of your lofty goals. Therefore, in order that you may accomplish the desires of your heavily burdened heart, it is my advice that you follow these instructions and reap the rewards that are justly due you.

Pour ten drops of Dragon's Blood Oil into your bath water, together with ten drops of Special Oil No. 20.

Dust your body daily with Jinks Removing Powder if you have been hurt or Algiers Powder if you are strong, and anoint your head also daily with Success Oil for good luck or Attraction Oil to draw a special desire.

Burn for one hour each day two small candles, a Green Candle for financial success, and a Pink Candle for the heartfelt friendship of others. Set the candles side by side, and around them lay many diverse coins. In front of these candles you should stand and recite the 23rd Psalm one time, leaving the candles to burn the remainder of the hour. Do this for six days.

On the seventh day, light no candle, but clean off the space and put the coins in the charity box, wrapped in a paper on which you have written a prayer for the advancement and abundance of all, from Psalms 66:12:

Thou hast caused men to ride over our heads; we went through fire and through water: but thou broughtest us out into a wealthy place.

The next day, again bathe, and dust, and anoint yourself, and begin again a cycle of six candles. And on the seventh day, give to the poor.

Do this three times in all, my dear child, with faith and constancy, and God will bless you and the spirit of success will smile upon you. So Be It.

14. THE MAN WHO WANTS THE SECRET OF PROSPERITY

O dear mother, it has always been a matter of wonder to me why, if all of God's children must sustain themselves with work, labour, and toil, some fall by the wayside and end in poverty while others succeed and enjoy the benefits of financial prosperity. I do not aspire to be wealthy, but if you know it, I humbly ask that you teach me the secret of prosperity, so that my family will never have to beg for help, and so that we may fully enjoy our lives.

My child, the Law of the Spirit is concrete. The Law of the Creator is concrete. The Law of Mankind is often questionable.

Prosperity is here for all to attain if approached in the proper and ethical way, with morality and conscience, fair play and decency.

Consideration, respect, and altruism give you purpose. Good humour, faith, benevolence, and sacrifice assist you through difficult times.

Prosperity can be yours, but it must be bought with fortitude and tenacity. Your inner strength must be matched by your ability to cooperate. Patience is also very important in the strenuous trek to prosperity.

Do the following things and help yourself on the way up.

Place a nine-inch Green Jumbo Candle in your house, anointed with Prosperity Oil and King Solomon Wisdom Oil. Rise early, before your habitual time for work, and burn the candle for one hour every day until it is consumed. During this hour, burn in your house a mixture of Good Luck Incense and Helping Hand Incense. And also during this hour, apply the Money Drawing Powder to your neck and chest daily, and clean your house each day, for one hour at a time, with Chinese Wash, until you have cleaned every room. And each day, at the conclusion of your hour of devotions, sit for a moment in silence. And when you pinch out the candle's flame, thank God for giving you the head, the hands, and the heart to do your work, and turn then to your daily occupations and do them well.

After this period of dedication, set aside time to light an octave of eight small Green Candles dressed with Prosperity and King Solomon Wisdom Oil, one every evening for eight evenings, and to rededicate yourself to your goal. And dress your head, your hands, and your heart with these oils as well.

And if you move to a new home, perform the same dedication there, so that it too will be a place for you to gain prosperity.

Stay out of too much debt. Do not become a slave to those who offer credit with interest. Protect your income. Good luck. So Be It.

15. THE MAN WHO WISHES TO ATTRACT ATTENTION

O dear mother, you see before you one who has great aspirations, but not yet great success. Unlike the many seekers who come before you, I am one who wishes to be well-known in this world. My aim is to appear before the public, and I believe myself skilled for the accomplishment of this desire.

The only thing that holds me back is a lack of attention. When I go before those who select the ones who will perform, I seem to lose my power to hold their eyes or ears. I feel diminished, and in the end I am given lesser parts to play, despite my best efforts. O mother, this is not vanity; it is my livelihood! How may I command the attention of those who hire the players, and draw the affection of the crowds who come to see the performances?

My friend, sometimes it seems as though everything is against us and whatever we attempt to do turns in the opposite direction. We find it very difficult to open the way or to straighten things out. When we almost reach our goal or our desire, something happens to upset our progress and the things we were reaching for disappear into nothing, leaving us in a state of want and despair. Here, my child, take it with more calm and faith, and fill your heart with hope. I will show you the way to attract attention.

Dissolve a spoonful of Dragon's Blood Bath Crystals in your bath water for luck. If you feel unsure of yourself, add a spoonful of Crucible of Courage Bath Crystals. If you are auditioning for a role and must win the part over others, add instead a spoonful of Victory Bath Crystals.

After the bath, anoint your head with Crown of Success Oil, lightly apply Look Me Over Oil to your face and body, and dress both your hands and the soles of your feet with Magnet Oil.

Array yourself in fair raiment and set out a triangle of small White Candles, each one anointed with one of the three oils. And at the center of the triangle of candles place a piece of jewelry that you will wear as a fascinator or lucky piece. It may be small and plain as long as it is well made. Dress it with the three oils and light the three candles around it. When the candles have finished burning, take up this lucky piece, hold it and pray for your desires. Then place it upon yourself, knowing that when you wear it, you will be blessed with the power of magnetic attraction.

Use Double Luck Perfume or Hoyt's Cologne as a regular perfume, wear your lucky piece where it will be seen, and may you find success. God bless you. So Be It.

16. THE MAN WHO WISHES TO INFLUENCE PEOPLE

O dear mother, although my lot in life has in many ways been good, I am one of those poor unfortunates who never is chosen to lead, but always must follow. This would not be so galling, but those who are placed above me treat me with contempt, and do not listen to my ideas, even when I know, through long experience, a better way to proceed. Instead, they speak to me as if I were lesser than them. Please help me to influence those who now despise me, so that they will treat me with respect and deference.

My child, you come to me because you seek help. You have been devoid of the power to influence those with whom you came in contact. It is written, my child, that you shall follow these instructions to gain the respect of your associates and thus accomplish your desire to lead and not to follow.

It is important that your body be clean at all times, as well as your raiment. Pour five drops of the Special Oil No. 20 and five drops of the Oil of Influence in your bath water. After bathing, apply to your body the Controlling Powder and rub on your hands and feet the Essence of Bend-Over Oil. Burn in your house a mixture of John the Conqueror Incense and Helping Hand Incense. Use the Master Oil as a perfume every day.

Burn a small White Candle every week dressed with each of these oils in turn: Special Oil No. 20, Influence, Essence of Bend-Over, and Master. At the close of one year, you will have burned 52 candles, or 13 of each type.

Remember as you do these things that it is the common lot of all to make enemies. The successful man or woman becomes so by transmuting enemies into friends; and mediocre men or women remain so because they not only make enemies, but keep them as such. Try to make a new friend each day and put forth a sincere effort to bind an old one closer to you.

Never, as long as you live, will you rid your life of disagreeable people, as long as you express the qualities which attract them. Avoid gossip, criticism, or passing derogatory remarks about anyone. When you eliminate these destructive states of thought, you will no longer have your life made miserable by offensive, obnoxious, and disgusting persons who seemingly live to annoy you and who always misunderstand you.

Express instead the emotions of love, truth, faith, gratitude, patience, and praise toward every condition, every circumstance, and every person in your life. Respect and influence will thus be yours and you will be a leader.

Do these things with faith and ask God to help you. So Be It.

Overcoming Financial Troubles

17. THE MAN WHO CANNOT FACE HIS DEBTS

O, good mother, I pray you hear your son in his deep misery, for I am beset with the landlord, the grocer, and the money lender. I am deeply in debt and cannot see a way to clear my debts. The landlord has sent me word that I will either pay him or he will set my goods out of doors. The grocer has said, "If you expect to get provisions, you must come to me with coins in hand for your credit is no longer accepted." And the money lender pursues me with the low sheriffs, besetting me even where I labour and where I dwell, so that I have no peace and am hounded at all times by him.

My dear son, your trials and tribulations have come to my ears and I have concern for you. So I will tell you how to appease the wrath of the landlord, the anger of the grocer, and the pursuit of the money lender.

The landlord you will meet with a good face and sweet words. Unfold to him the story of the money lender, and he will give you advice. But you must also help yourself in his eyes by giving him a small amount of silver. When he comes, sprinkle upon your clothing the Oil of Bend-Over, in which you have soaked Yellow Dock Root, Sampson Snake Root and White Flowers of the Field, so that he will hearken unto you and his mind will be set to help you and he will believe you and give you more time in your house.

The grocer you will go unto and speak smoothly and give him great promises, and while you are speaking to him you will have in your mouth the Wish Bean or Mojo Bean. This you will chew and spit out the hulls in and around the store so that the keeper will do as you wish and give you more provisions and more time in which to pay him.

And for the money lender, you will take the advice of your landlord and also obtain nine small Blue Candles, and these you will burn, one every night for nine nights, as a novena, and under them as they burn you will put the name of the money lender so that he will lose the power to do you harm. And you will go to the money lender and say "Lo, I have paid you in interest twice the amount you loaned me and now you have two pieces of silver where only one was before, and this is enough for you," and then, as you go out of his presence, you will let fall from your hand the Powder of Perdition so that he will lose some of the money he already has. So Be It.

18. THE LADY WHO CANNOT FACE HER LANDLORD

O dear mother, I come before you heavily burdened and filled with dread, for through no fault of my own, I was sick and could not work, and thus I fell short in my accounts, and it has now come time to pay the landlord, and I do not have the money, nor do my family or friends have any to lend me. I am working now to earn what I missed, but today I have it not.

O mother, I know I am in the wrong, and my landlord is in the right, but I cannot face him until I shall have the funds to pay him, for fear he will dispossess me of my dwelling.

O my daughter, you who come to me in your trouble and lay down your burden at the feet of the God of Peace and Plenty, you who come to me for advice and comfort, I say unto you, you shall sprinkle your raiment with a great help. You shall sprinkle it on your sleeves and your bodice, and you shall rub your hands with it, the liquid made of Yellow Dock Root, Sampson Snake Root, and the Oil of Carnation Flowers with the Essence of Bend-Over. And you shall pray the following prayer:

O Lord of Pity, O Lord of Comfort, look down upon your daughter and open the everlasting well of your goodness and change the heart of [name of the landlord] so that he will forgive what I owe him until the debt is repaid. And for worship to yourself I bind myself and truly promise that each night for nine nights, as the stars rise in the heavens, I will burn a candle of Peace, of pure white wax, to your memory and in thanks for the goodness received from your hands.

O my daughter, you will keep your promise you made to the God of Pity and Compassion by burning one White Candle every night with the name of your landlord beneath your own, on a strip of parchment paper, thus:

(Your Name)

(Your Landlord's Name)

Each candle you will dress with Peaceful Home Oil and you will put the paper under it so that the wax will flow on it, and bear in mind and be of good judgement that the candle does not go out until it shall be consumed.

And it shall so happen that when the landlord shall come to you, you shall receive him with kind words and a smooth tongue and tell him of your sickness and your tribulations, and ask him to bear with you and have compassion, until the God of Pity and Compassion dwells in his breast.

O my daughter, go in peace and abide in plenty. So Be It.

19. THE MAN WHO HAS DIFFICULTIES ON THE JOB

O good mother, look down on your son, as he is in deep trouble and cannot see his way for the darkness that surrounds him. It has been whispered to me that I have been crossed at my job, and indeed, nothing seems to go well with me, and all of my undertakings go wrong.

The head man of my work does not like me, and all of the worst and the hardest labours are put on my shoulders, and even then he is never pleased, no matter all that I do to try to earn his good word. When I ask for a chance to work longer hours, I am put off and excused. The head man cannot find work for me, but it seems easy to find work for others.

O my son, be light of heart and do not let the dark clouds which surround you bear you down, for no matter how dark it looks, there is always a way that will give you help.

To untie yourself, you will gather together nine threads of pure silk, the length of your body from feet to head, and you will tie nine knots in this at equal distance to make a knotted string. This you will wear upon your body for nine days, and for every day of the nine days you will burn Frankincense and Myrrh before a picture of Saint Joseph the Worker. And on the last of the nine days, remove the string of silk which you have been wearing and burn it along with Frankincense and Myrrh on that day. And be sure that all the knots are burned, so that you will be untied and free again.

It is also said that if you wear around your neck a finger of the Root called the Wonder of the World, tied with a thread, this will give you luck on the job, particularly if you write the name of the head man on it.

And when you go to the head man to ask him for longer hours or lighter work, you will have with you some of the Saint Joseph Wish Beans, and he will hearken unto you and give you the task you wish for and pay you fairly for your labour.

And on your raiment you will have a few drops of the Oil of Saint Joseph, so that all of the evil spirits at the work site will be driven from you and only the good spirits will commune with you and give you good thoughts, and they will tell you what is best for you to do.

And at all times remember well that the good workman is worthy of his hire. Do your duty well and faithfully and you will be looked up to and respected by the ones with whom you labour, as well as those you serve. For this way only is the true way and free road to prosperity. So Be It.

20. THE LADY WHO HAS AN EMPTY BOARDING HOUSE

O good mother, I come to you to ask your help, for prosperity and plenty are not with me. My boarding house is empty. There is no laughter, nor are there any feast days. The people pass my door and see me not, neither do they stop nor look into my inn, for they do not remember me nor seek to know me. The clink of gold has not passed my palm for these many days, neither friends nor strangers have brought me gifts, and my purse hangs limp with no hopes of having it filled. O good mother, I am full of lamentations and it seems that the evil spirits live in my house, so I beg that you shall hear my prayer and in your wisdom give me help.

My poor helpless daughter, in the fullness of my heart I will assist you to make prosperity smile on you, that you will have again feast days and a full house, and your raiment shall be of many hues and fine texture, and it shall reflect your prosperity.

Into the corner of each room of your house and at the front door you will put the Magnetic Sand, and you will put into your scrub water, on the day you dress up your house before the end of the week, the Essence of Fast Luck and with this you will cleanse the floors on the day before the Sabbath.

Then, in the hallway and the by-ways of your house you will burn, for the next five days, the Incense of Saint Joseph with Frankincense, Myrrh, Cedarwood, and Sandalwood, so that the fumes and perfumes thereof will penetrate all of your home, driving out the evil spirits and bringing in the good. And the ashes you will throw in your backyard after each burning.

On the sixth day that you burn of this mixture you will also put into it Dragon's Blood resin for luck, and by the front door you will put the pictures of Saint Christopher and Saint Raphæl, and by the back door you will put their pictures also, so that when travellers enter into your house, they will find good companions and will remain and will not leave.

And when the seventh day comes, in the morning you will dress up your house, and you will take of the Salt of Saint Peter, called Salt Peter, and sprinkle your house with it so that those who have entered into your house during the six days will remain, and the good spirits will remain as well, and all will be of one mind.

Do these things so that strangers, friends, and helpful spirits shall enter and shall shower you with kindness and worldly goods, and prosperity shall enter and drive away care and worry. So Be It.

21. THE MAN WHOSE BUSINESS IS POOR

O dear mother, I pray you to come to my rescue as I am almost to my last resort and my last shekel, for all of my good business is gone from me and my pockets are not heavy with gold and silver like in the olden days.

When strangers step in my place of business it seems as if I cannot please them with my goods or with my sweet words, and they walk out empty-handed. Where many pieces of silver once changed hands, now there is only silence. My goods remain on my shelves until they are spoiled and I cannot even get what the merchant prince has asked me to pay for them.

Good mother, if I do not soon get help and bring once more the sound of silver to my purse, I will be set upon by the money lenders and the sheriff and only woe will be my lot and gone will be my house of business. Good mother, I appeal to you for help. Pray hear my cries of distress.

My good son, I have heard your plea and I think that God will help you in your need and show you the way of good business and new customers, and also make some of your old customers come back to you to do as in the old days. First you will have to pacify the spirit of prosperity as follows:

Take the Jinks Removing Sprinkling Salt and sprinkle it on the front part of your business. Place it outside the door, that people may walk on or over it without noticing it, and when you have closed up for the night, then you will burn together the Incenses of John the Conqueror, Attraction, and Good Luck, allowing the fumes to penetrate every corner of the place.

And for yourself, you will take the Root of John the Conqueror and put it in your pocket, and when you get up in the morning, before opening the door for business, the first thing you will do will be to put three drops of the Lucky Lodestone Perfume on the John the Conqueror Root, so that it will attract money and you will have the power of talking to your customers that they will buy your goods. But be sure that once you have made the John the Conqueror Root work for you, no other human hand shall touch it, except yours, so that the power of attraction shall be for you and no other.

And my child, be sure that you treat your customers with consideration and with honesty, and always have the kindness of your heart showing on your face so that they will come unto you and give you confidence and respect. Herein fail not, as the spirit of prosperity will not continue to smile on you if you do not heed this advice, for the spirit of prosperity has two heads and can speak good and evil at the same time. So Be It.

22. THE LADY WHO LOST HER BUSINESS

O good mother, your daughter comes to you on bending knees to ask for a great favour, for where there was light and laughter, now there is only silence. Where many feet wore out the threshold of my front door, now scarcely anyone enters, and where gold coursed in a steady stream, not even a shekel is now seen. No gold or silver come to me. My goods remain in my storehouse, with no one to buy or even ask the price thereof. So, good mother, if I do not soon get help and if you do not hear my prayer, the sheriff and his minions will soon enter my household and my storehouse and take from me what I have left to sell.

O my daughter, it is said that "she who has, shall be given again;" so to make that come to pass you will take of the Steel Dust and the Powder of the Cinnamon and of the Wonder of the World Root. These you will mix together and separate them into four packets and you will put one of them in each of the four corners of the room wherein your business is done. This is said by the spirits to make the mind follow your goods, so that the stranger will buy from you and money will again pass the palm of your hands.

And you will put into the pocket wherein you put your hand the most, a silver Mercury Dime, so that when you speak, the customers will hearken unto you and believe you and have a great desire to get your merchandise.

You will put into the water with which you wash your storehouse floor the Lucky Blueing Powder, and with this you will scrub the floor.

You will mix Frankincense and Myrrh with Allspice Berries and the flowers of Lavender, and this offering you will burn on Charcoal every day in your storehouse, so that the spirits of contention and strife will leave and only good spirits of friendship and help will remain within.

And to return to you that which was lost, by the front door you will put a picture of Saint Anthony so that faith will enter, and by the back door you will put a picture of Saint Anthony so that faith will not depart. Before these you will set Seeds of Paradise, which will raise you to safety and plenty.

Herein fail not, my daughter, to do faithfully each of these things so that prosperity will again smile on you and you will wear beautiful raiment and you will jingle much gold and silver in your purse, so that the stranger and the friend will come unto you and say, "Lo, I am much pleased, sell unto me again of your merchandise; here, take my gold, for I would show my gratitude, and let the music begin, for I am happy in your house." So Be It.

Overcoming Love Troubles

23. THE MAN WHO CANNOT GET A SWEETHEART

O dear mother, I ask your good and wholesome advice, for I don't seem to have any luck to get a sweetheart. I see them once and speak to them, but when I go back the second time, their encouragement has gone. I meet them at parties and have a good time with them, but when I ask to call upon them, they turn a deaf ear to me. I meet them in company and am made welcome, but when I wish to commune with them privately, their excuses are many. I can make no headway in my love affairs.

O mother, my heart yearns for a sweetheart and it would be my complete happiness if I could make one understand me and love me in return.

My son, I am glad you have come to me for advice, for many more good sons of mine come not to me and therefore are not happy.

In order that you may be blessed, in the water in which you bathe you will put every day for three weeks five drops of the Black Cat Perfume Oil to attract to you the spirit of love, and it will help you to gain your desires.

And in your room you will burn John the Conqueror Incense every day.

And you will get of the Peace Water and sprinkle it in front of the house wherein lives the lady of your choice. Sprinkle it in such a manner that she will step on it or over it. You will do this for three nights after dark when no one will see you, and be sure that you step over it when you go in to see her.

And when going to see her, you will sprinkle on your garments the Love Oil. And on your skin you will use the Love Powder, so that she will listen to your words. You will tell her how beautiful she is and how sweet is her voice when she speaks, and you will impress upon her mind that you think very much of her. And in case you cannot see her or speak to her, then you will sit yourself down and write her a letter praising her and speaking of her beauty, and before you seal this letter you will put a few drops of the Hoyt's Cologne around the edge of the paper.

And when you are well acquainted with her, but not before then, you will put some of the Kiss Me Now Powder on her garments so that her love for you will grow warmer and she will never turn from you or forget you.

So my son, do all of these things to get the help of God and to attract the spirit of love, that your sweetheart will give you many happy days. So Be It.

24. THE LADY WHO HAS A LOVE-RIVAL

My good mother, I come to you with a troubled mind, for I love where I am not loved in return. My sweetheart has been captured by the flirtations of my rival, a woman whom he has known for many years, and who uses wicked ways to turn him away from me. The thought of losing him has driven me to despair. O mother, please help me!

My daughter, the evil work of your rival has cloaked you in gloom, but charms of love are prepared in the spirit of hope, and so to begin, you must remove all of your black clothing. Nothing must be crossed, neither your feet nor your hands. For fear two pins might cross in your hair, it is best to take them out. Write your name, your lover's name, and your rival's name each on a slip of paper, letting no one see them but you. Your rival's name you will soak in a dish of Vinegar, Salt, and Black Pepper, and after three days you will throw them into running water, but the papers of yourself and your beloved you will drop into a bowl of burning whiskey.

Next you will carve seven notches in a Blue Candle and burn it seven nights in your bedroom, from notch to notch, reciting three Hail Marys as each portion burns. And you will put five Guinea Grains in your mouth whenever your lover comes near, to soften him toward you.

And when your lover first enters your house, go to your kitchen and prepare a glass of sugared water, very sweet, and with it Sweet Basil, and throw it in the yard with your back toward the street. Feed him two Apples to make him love you, and two candies to make him sweet to you.

With Guinea Grains and Cloves in your mouth, you can get anything you want from your man. If you place one of his hairs where water drips upon it, you will bring him under your command, and if you conceal a Lodestone near where you sit with him, you will give him ambition.

For protection from your rival, buy 19 Red Candles for Saint Michæl. Light one on the first Monday and one on the first Friday of each month, dressed with his Oil, and before it set three saucers, one with Honey, one with Holy Water, and one with Orange Flower Water. And on the second Friday of each month pray to Saint Roch at three o'clock and make your wish.

To destroy your rival, get hold of some piece of her garments, and cut it and sew it, and she will not live to wear it again. And you may rub her picture with Graveyard Dirt from the grave of a murderer and carry the picture upside down in your pocket and she will surely die. So be it.

25. THE MAN WHO LOST HIS SWEETHEART

O dear mother, you see your son before you with tears in his eyes and a downcast look in his face, for I have lost my beautiful sweetheart whom I have loved for many a day and whom I cannot forget. She is always in my mind and I cannot sleep for the thoughts of her. Her beautiful face is always before me, in my waking hours and in my hours of labour. I would gladly give half my life for another moment of happiness with her. O mother, hear my prayer and help me.

My poor son, I hearken to your words of sorrow and gladly extend my help that you may smile again and that you will again be glad to see the streak of daylight break the skies, that your tears will stop their flow, and you will be yourself again with your sweetheart at your side.

Lo, you will send to your sweetheart a box of sweets and with it one dozen blooms of the Pink Rose of Damascus. In your bath water you will pour ten drops of Special Oil No. 20. Then you will call upon her at her place of abode so that you may speak sweet words to her, and you will have upon your raiment the Oil of Attraction. And in your shoes, you will put the Powder of Attraction so that she will be willing to speak to you and hearken to your words of gentle passion. And let it come to pass that you shall put some of the Oil of Attraction upon her, and to accomplish this you must use your wits and your persuasion. This will make her think of you while you are gone from her presence.

But if she will not see you, then you will write her a letter of sweet words with promises of better times and in this letter you will sprinkle of the Powder of Return To Me so that she will agree to see you again.

And if she still does not return, you will make a novena of Pink Candles, one each for nine days, and under each candle you will put her name so that the wax will flow upon it and cover it. And behind the candles hang a picture of Our Lady of the Sacred Heart, and she will help you in your sorrow.

And after you get your sweetheart to come to you, you will take the Love Powder and put it in her shoe or on her powder puff in a way that she will not see or notice it; this you will do to increase her love for you and that her mind will not change and that she will remain with you to her last day.

And be sure when you get her back that you treat her with kindness and be true to her so that her love for you shall grow stronger, and she shall have thoughts of no one else but you. So Be It.

26. THE LADY WHO LOST HER LOVER

Good mother, the man of my heart has left me. He does not come to my house and tell me of his love. He passes me by without any smile on his face. His eyes no longer sparkle with love when he speaks to me. His heart is cold to all of my advances. He has eyes for other women. I have no longer the power to hold his tender thoughts. He listens to the voices of the sirens and does not harken unto me.

O good mother, I come unto you in deep distress and poor in spirit. I beg for your help that I may be comforted and loved, just as in the days gone by, and that my loved one may remain by my side, for all of the beauty and sunshine have gone from my life.

My poor downcast daughter, it is with deep feeling and regard that I hear of your great pains and tribulations, but it is written that the Sun shall again shine for you in gladness.

To accomplish this great desire, you will take the Buds from the Garden of Gilead and make a package of them, and upon this you will put of the Essence of Van Van. This you will put in the raiment of the one you love. And if that be not possible, you shall make a small token of your skill — some token with which he shall adorn his person. This you shall give him.

Each day in your bath you shall put a few drops of the Oil No. 20, and use the Return To Me Powder on your bosom every day.

And you shall make a small altar in your private room, and on it put a holy picture of Mary, and before it you shall burn the Incense of the Temple of Solomon every day, praying that your charms will cause your loved one to think deeply of you and that you shall never be absent from his mind.

And before this altar you will burn nine Pink Candles while the Sun is up in the heavens, lighting one of the candles every day for nine days, and under the candle-stand you will put a piece of parchment paper on which you will write the name of the one you love so that the wax will cover his name, even dripping the wax on his name by design, so that no one can get his name but yourself. And you will recite the 45th Psalm for love.

And when you shall seek your loved one you shall not upbraid him, neither shall you talk disapprovingly of him; but you shall smile on him and you shall be friendly and true to him. You will do all of these things, and you will be of good cheer and pure purpose so that God shall smile on your work, and your life shall be only beauty and sunshine. So Be It.

27. THE MAN WHOSE WIFE LEFT HOME

Dear mother, the woman of my heart has left my roof and I have no peace or rest. She has gone from me with very few words and I am broken-hearted, for I have her always in my mind.

Tales have come to my ears that she left me for another man whom she loves better than she does me. Other tales are told that she left only because she does not love me any more, as she used to do in the long ago.

I do not know what to do or whom to believe. I come to you that you may quiet my mind and make her think of me often and make her come back to me and love me in the same old way as she did before.

My dear son, your heart-broken story has come to me and I hasten to answer your prayer that you may take your place again in the house of happiness, for love is the foundation of all things and love rules the world.

In order that you may win back the love of your wife and in order that she will come back to you, you will do the following things:

If you still live in the same house where you once dwelt in happiness with your woman, then all around the house you will sprinkle Magnetic Sand, and you will scrub the floors with Rosemary, Rose, and Lovage Oils mixed in equal portions, using twenty drops of the mixture in your scrubbing water.

But if you have moved and you want her to follow you to your new home, then all around the location of the old house you will sprinkle Magnetic Sand, and with it you will also draw a path to your new house, either walking or riding, sprinkling Magnetic Sand at every crossroads along the way, and then all around your new home. And you will scrub the floor of your room with the Oils of Rosemary, Roses, and Lovage mixed in equal portions, using twenty drops of the mixture in your scrubbing water.

And you will go to see her and upon your clothes you will sprinkle of the Oil of Reconciliation close to your body, and you will speak to her with sweet words and many promises, that she will believe you and follow you.

And if you cannot see her where she dwells now, then you will write her a letter of love and forgiveness and on that letter, you will put two drops of the Oil of Bend-Over, so that she will read the words and believe them.

And in your house you will burn a novena of nine Red Candles blessed with all five oils, one each night for nine nights, so that the flames of love shall be rekindled and shall burn again, and under these candles you will put her name, so that the wax shall fall over it as the candles burn. So Be It.

28. THE LADY WHOSE HUSBAND LEFT HOME

O good mother, I come unto you in deep distress. Tears have coursed my face in the dark hours of the night, for he who was the companion of my soul — my dear husband — has left our home and gone from my side, gone where my cries of distress will not reach him, where my tender words will not be heard by him, and where the sirens and bad women will have sway over him and make him forget me forever.

He is gone where I cannot minister unto him nor show my love. He has left me desolate and alone. Darkness closes in about me and drags me down to the depths. O mother, I cannot live apart from him. I am sorely pressed and can only ask for death, without your help.

O my good daughter, do not lose hope and faith, for the stars say that there is a way to make your loved one's spirit commune with you and to have him come back to your side, there to remain and to comfort and protect you. In order to accomplish this, you will bring your troubles to the attention of the good spirits and get their help, and they will stop the work of the spirits of ill omen, and you will again find happiness.

You will bring into your home a Horseshoe Magnet, red in the center and bright on the ends, and you will get a packet of Magnetic Sand, and this you will pour on the bright ends of the Magnet so that some will remain on it.

This you will lay upon your altar to attract his love again, and his worldly goods shall remain with you. And in the center of it you will place a candle stand and there burn a novena of nine Pink Candles, with his name under each one so that they will be for him only. One of them you will burn each day before the time he would have come home to the house. And you will wear a pink and gold garter of Saint Martha on your left leg and let no one but your loved one touch it. And if he does not come, you will write him a good letter, and on it sprinkle Return To Me Powder so he will think of you.

If, for reasons known to you only, you wish he should become jealous of you, to your advantage, it is written that a novena made of nine Green Candles shall help you, if under each candle you will put your name and his name together, written on a piece of pure parchment paper. One of these you will burn each night for nine nights. This will make the green-eyed monster of jealousy enter his mind and he will think of you both night and day, and he shall stay awake in the dark hours of the night and envision you.

Herein fail not, for your happiness and love depend upon it. So Be It.

Overcoming Family Troubles

29. THE MAN WHOSE CHILDREN DO NOT HELP HIM

O mother, all my life I worked to aid and assist my beloved wife and our children. I was strong, and I supported them in every way. Now my wife has passed away and I am alone. I am grown old and my heart is breaking because my children come here no more. O mother, how can I draw my wandering children back, that they may help me in my aged years and I may leave them my property in good array and with a loving heart?

My dear son, I hear and understand your sorrowful plea.

You will take of the Root of the Rattlesnake and the Oil of Sassafras. The oil you will sprinkle on the root and then you will make four bundles of it, and one of these bundles you will put in each corner of the home so that the evil spirits of the four winds will not be able to abide there any more.

And you will put a picture of the Holy Saint Joseph in the room wherein you take your rest, and before this holy saint you will burn a Blue Candle every day until the spirit of God enters the hearts of your children. And as the candle burns, you will pray to Joseph that he intercede for you in the hearts of your children so they will do those things which are their duty.

And in the clothing of your children you will put the Essence of Influence, if you can get to their clothing; and if you cannot, then you will write them a loving letter and sprinkle some Powder of Influence onto the letter, and send it to them so that it will get into their hands as they open it.

And you will take of the Holy Water and mix with it the Oil of Cedar of Lebanon and Essence of Amber; this you will put on your clothes when you see your children, so that they can see your sorrow and they in their turn be sorry for you. And a great pity shall swell up in their hearts for you.

And if you visit in their house, you will burn the Red Devil's Incense, a pinch every day for nine days in your room there, and you will not open the door until the smoke has penetrated into the four corners of the room.

But also remember at all times that you yourself must never lose the love you bear for your children, for if you do, then your sin will be even greater than theirs and you will not succeed in your undertaking, for no matter what they may do or say against you, still it is your duty to love and protect them even unto the last day of your life. So Be It.

30. THE WOMAN WHOSE CHILDREN ARE UNGRATEFUL

O my good mother, with tears in my eyes and my heart broken with grief, I come to you in distress, for the flesh of my flesh, the blood of my blood, and the bones of my bones have gone against me.

My own dear children have turned their faces from me and have ceased loving me. Instead of their fondness, I have cold sneering words; instead of their caresses, I have rough actions. They do not ask me for advice, but instead do things they know are against my wishes. Instead of praising me, they let me know that all of my actions displease them. Ingratitude is in their eyes, their actions, and their words.

O good mother, help me, I beseech you.

O my daughter, I have painfully heard your prayer, for the love of the mother is eternal, while the love of the lover is passing, and the love of the friend is changing and quickly forgotten. Be you of good cheer and stout heart, for the help of God is with you and the help of all the good spirits and the great angels is for you. And they shall see that you fail not in your undertaking. So my poor daughter, these things you will do to enlist their attention, and the help of God, and the good spirits, and the high angels.

In your front room wherein you take your rest, you will put the picture of Mary, the Virgin Mother, with the Child, and you will ask her help while burning in front of her every day Frankincense and Myrrh. And every week you will also burn before her one Pink Candle of pure wax. And under the stand on which you place the candle you will put the name of each child you wish to lovingly come back to your arms, and you will bear with each child and have patience, and speak as mildly as Mary spoke to Jesus.

And you will carry a Queen Elizabeth Root and on your raiment you will put the Essence of Geranium mixed with the Essence of Roses, renewing it in the evening when your children come in from the schools or the fields or from labour, so that they will seek you out and be pleased. Neither will you upbraid them in sorrow, but always welcome them lovingly.

And on the days you wash your house, you shall boil water with Rosemary leaves and Basil leaves. And the leaves you will scatter outside, about the house, but the infused water you will add to warm water with Ivory Soap, to which you also add a few drops of Peace Water, and this you will use as a floor wash, as you pray Psalms 133 for mutual affection.

It is your blood which speaks and you shall forgive them. So Be It.

31. THE MAN WHO WANTS PEACE IN HIS HOME

O good mother, my home, once a sanctuary of peace, has become a place of anger, harsh words, conflict, and dismay. The atmosphere is one of tension and sorrow, and those who used to dwell in happy accord and agreement, and who delighted in the simple pleasures of family life, now speak to one another only to find fault or remain in cold silence and plan to go their separate ways.

Good mother, it may be that enemies have brought unrest to us out of jealousy, or it may be that an evil spirit has come to dwell among us. The air in the home seems darker by the day, and tears have been shed in every room. Without peace in our home, I feel that we must perish. Please, mother, help me to bring about better times in my home.

My friend, you come to me with tears in your eyes and your heart filled with worries over the condition of your home. Where there should be harmony, love, understanding, and peace, only sadness and disappointment fill the atmosphere. It is my advice, dear friend, that you follow these instructions and bring sunshine into your home.

Sprinkle Jinks Killer Salt around the outside of the house to keep off unpleasant visitors or spirits. Open all of your doors and windows and pray for evil to depart. Burn the John the Conqueror Incense mixed with the Helping Hand Incense, carrying it from room to room until every room has been freshened with it. Close the doors and windows and sprinkle every room of your house with Peace Water, reciting Psalms 122: 7-8:

Peace be within thy walls, and prosperity within thy palaces. For my brethren and companions' sakes, I will now say, Peace be within thee.

Apply to your body daily the Peaceful Home Powder, that tranquility will ensue. Anoint your head and feet daily with the Bend-Over Drops, that others in the home will cease their plans to argue or to separate.

Burn for one hour each day or night a White Candle dressed with House Blessing Oil, until you have burned three of them.

Cook daily any such foods as you wish that may include either Basil and Rosemary, for peace and domestic harmony; or Sugar, Vanilla, Cinnamon, and Cloves, for sweetness, love, and luck.

Do these things, my dear child, and let no frown be reflected on your face, but keep your mind fixed on unity and harmony.

Peace be with you. So Be It.

32. THE WOMAN WHOSE CHILDREN ARE IN TROUBLE

O my good mother, I pray you to help me, to give me strength, and to protect me from the trouble that has befallen my house, for my own children have become as strangers and enemies to me. They whisper that I may soon be dead so that they may do as they please and divide my worldly goods between them. They covet my raiment, my jewels, and my household goods. They know no respect and kindness towards me.

They take the veriest stranger for their friend, while they take me for their enemy. They go from home in the hours of darkness and come not again until the break of day. Their companions, instead of being meek, pure, and righteous, are noisy, vile, and insulting, and lead them into unclean ways. They follow after one who coaxes them into disrepute, and I fear that if they do not soon mend their ways, they will be taken by the high sheriff and brought before a harsh judge, and I will see them no more.

Dear daughter, I hear the words of your broken mother's heart. Your children follow evil, and I say unto you that those who led them astray shall be punished if they do not come in meekness and ask your forgiveness.

In your house, in each corner of every room, you will place a Bay Leaf on which you have written the word *"Peace,"* and on it put the Powder of Wonder of the World Root. And on these, in each corner, you shall sprinkle Salt, and pray for protection and peace. And after three days, take them up and burn them with Frankincense and Myrrh upon a bed of Charcoal.

And in the shoe or raiment of the wicked one who is the leader among your children you will put of the Powder called Confusion, so that, as at the Tower of Babel, this child will confuse those to whom he would give advice and he will not be believed. But those who hear him shall say, "Liar and blasphemer, be gone from me, for the truth is not in you and you shall be cursed and shall be damned for every day that the Sun shall shine on you."

But your own children's clothing you shall wash with Peace Water.

And if this wicked child with the poisoned tongue shall be taken by the law, then you shall burn a novena of nine Black Candles, one every day for nine days, with his name under each one. And let the wax run down on his name, and cover it with Black Pepper. And you shall pray to God every day for nine days, as the candles burn, that he shall heap ill luck and sickness upon his own head until he shall repent and ask your forgiveness and your ministrations, and these shall you give freely if you are asked. So Be It.

Overcoming Legal Troubles

33. THE COURT SCRAPE, OR THE LADY GOING TO TRIAL

O good mother, I am sore of feet and heavy of heart, for the power of man has said that I shall be put in the darkest dungeon and that I shall be deprived of the beauty, pleasures, and good will of the world, that my friends shall look down on me, that they shall show displeasure and pass me with their faces turned away, and that my enemies will vilify me and say untruths and blasphemy and perjury, to my dismay, so that they can point their fingers at me, and pass me in the streets of the city, and heap scorn on the heads of those dear to me and those who love me.

O daughter, I say unto you that you shall come with your law man before the judges and the scribes and they will pass judgement upon you, and according to your faith and hope, you shall be judged, and according to your sacrifices and invocations, you shall be judged, and according to the wise counsels and smooth tongues of those who assist you, you shall be judged.

My child, to cool the wrath of God, you shall take the Root of the Little or Low John to Chew and dried Dragon's Blood, and upon these you shall sprinkle a drop of Dove's Blood Oil and wrap them in bright coloured tissue and put them in the farthest corner of your house or behind your bed so that no hand shall touch them. There they shall remain for nine days.

And you shall make a novena of nine Brown Candles and burn one every day with Victory Oil with the names of your helpers under them. And you shall make a novena of nine Black Candles and burn one every day with Destruction Oil and the names of your enemies under them, written in very small letters. And you shall burn them side by side, so that the waxes will not mix. For the brown are for victory and the black are for conquering enemies.

And at the end of the nine days you shall take up the packet that you made and add to it the beans called Wish Beans and carry it in Red Flannel every day, allowing no one to touch it but yourself. On the day of the trial, you shall take a new, dry piece of the Low John Root and chew it as you enter the court room and you shall spit the finely chewed root inside the room, allowing no one to see you do it, so that the judge shall hearken unto the testimony of your friends and hear with pleasure the words of your witnesses and believe them, and he shall deal with you mildly. So Be It.

34. THE MAN WHO IS PURSUED BY THE LAW

O good mother, the law of the land is on my trail and I am compelled to hide myself away from the eyes of the sheriff and the bailiff, for they seek me at all times, in all places. I dare not walk in the streets for fear that I will be put in the dungeon and kept there for a long space of time away from the sunshine and smiles of the outer world. I have been accused of all sorts of things which are against the law of the land and at all hours of the day and night I am searched for and hounded so that I have no peace. I do not know who is my friend and who are my enemies. My mind is uncertain, my life is in danger, and I know not whether I will see the Sun rise or the good Moon go down behind the clouds from one day to the next.

My poor son, I hear your cries of anguish and hasten to give you advice that the blight may be taken from you and you may walk the streets in peace.

You will take the Big John the Conqueror Root and also the Black Snake Root, and powder them, and of this you will make a small package inside a White Handkerchief, and on this you will drip the Oil of Wintergreen. This you will keep on yourself at all times until danger is past. Fail not to see that no human hand but yours touches it after you have let it touch your body.

To make your enemies leave, so that they will not come back, take Hot Foot Powder and sprinkle where your enemies walk, or put it in their shoes.

And so that the sheriff and his law men will not think of you, you will give them sickness and trouble of their own. You will burn a novena of nine Black Candles dipped in Holy Oil and rolled in Graveyard Dirt, lighting them upside down, one every night for nine nights, just as the Sun goes down. And as they burn, you will pray to God and ask his help to overcome your enemies and have peace and happiness for your own.

And if the sheriffs have already taken you before the learned judge, you will take of the Dove's Blood Ink and write with it:

O pure blood without sin, like the pure white dove that you represent, make me pure in the eyes of men and make it so that the judges shall see only purity and no sin, and that I shall be made whole again.

This must be written on pure parchment paper and after reading it over to yourself on your knees, it is to be burned and the ashes scattered.

This you will do every time you get a paper commanding you to appear before the judges. Obey their commands, but also fail not in carrying out this covenant if you value your life and liberty. So Be It.

35. THE LADY IN THE LAWSUIT

O good mother, I am on my knees before you to pray for help, as I am deeply troubled and persecuted by my enemies. One says, "Lo, this woman has made war on us and caused disturbances in our family." Another says, "This woman has taken weapons of war and has attempted to spill my life's blood." And still another says, "This woman has entered my house when I was away doing my labour in the fields and taken my worldly goods."

O good mother, now the learned judge and the high sheriff and the men of the law have threatened to put me in the dungeon where there is no light and the vermin crawl over you and eat out your heart, where only gloom will be my companion, where I will never see the face of the Sun.

O good mother, help your downtrodden daughter.

My poor daughter, I hear your prayer and will hasten to your help with heartfelt sympathy and tell you the secrets of the learned judges so that you can conquer your enemies and once more breathe the air of freedom, so that the Sun shall shine on your head and bring you comfort, so that the good Moon shall bring you peace and smile on your face.

You shall take the herb Goldenseal and the Sachet of Geranium and put them together and wrap them up in the paper of the court when the low sheriff brings it to you, so that the power to soothe the anger of the law will be worked on it until the time comes when you shall come before the judge.

And you shall place the picture of Jesus the Just Judge by your front door and sprinkle in every corner Peace Water. And around your neck you shall wear a scapular of the Lamb of God, and in your purse carry the Low John Root and allow no one to touch it until your troubles shall be over.

And you shall burn a novena of nine Black Candles upside down, one every day for nine days, after the Sun has gone down, and under them place a paper with the names of your enemies on it, also upside down, and sprinkle it with Cayenne Powder and Poppy Seeds so that their testimony will not be believed and they will become confused when they speak to the judge.

And the night before you are to appear in court, you will burn three White Candles with Court Case Oil, in a triangle around the court papers, and you will also burn the Oriental Incense of the great King Solomon to give your lawyer wisdom to seek the mercy of the judge, so that you may be set free.

My daughter, do you all of these things so that you can triumph over your enemies and have power and happiness. So Be It.

36. THE MAN WHOSE LODGE BROTHERS GAINSAY HIM

O mother, I have long been a member in good standing of a noble lodge of brothers, but after years of faithful trust, a slanderous member spread the claim that I am a thief. My brothers do not greet me with smiles as once they did. When I seek a favour, I am denied, and behind my back, untruths are said. They threaten to have me up on charges. O mother, how may I overcome this?

My son, as you go into the lodge and the Guard of the Outer Chamber challenges you, give him the proper word and at the same time sprinkle some of the Controlling Powders at the door just before he opens it, so that he will be your friend and tell you news that is of some benefit to you.

Then, as you walk into the sanctum and get to the Inner Guard, and you are challenged, you will again give the proper word and at the same time you will sprinkle some of the Goofer Dust around the door as he opens it, to kill the evil plans of those who have falsely accused you.

And when you enter the lodge room, you will have in your pocket, folded in a White Handkerchief so that no one may handle it after you have once touched it. the Eye of the Cat, a piece of Ruler's Root, and Psalms 133:

Behold, how good and how pleasant it is for brethren to dwell together in unity!

This you yourself will not touch until you are ready to address the Grand Master to ask for something to your advantage. Then, when you speak, you will keep the packet in your hand so that the Eye of the Cat will see far and make out hidden things, the Ruler's Root will bring your brothers back to your way of thinking, and the Psalms will support you among them all.

And, my son, bear with those who wish you ill and speak not too badly of them, but tell the whole truth always. And to all of your brothers, give a glad hand and speak pleasantly, for he who smiles not, but wears a scowl on his face will surely not attract unto himself the good wishes and the helpful ways of the others. It is only he who has a friendly spirit who draws his brothers to him and makes them his brothers in truth. And for any particular brother with whom you wish to get well acquainted and become more friendly, you will take a cigar, and put two drops of pure Oil of Rose of Damascus into it, and make a gift of it, to attract his good will.

So now, my son, go your way and treat others with good cheer and honest purpose, so the charges will be set aside, and you will be honoured in your day and remembered after the cold grave closes upon you. So Be It.

Overcoming Social Troubles

37. THE MAN WHOSE LADY FRIENDS SPEAK BADLY OF HIM

O good mother, look into your son's upturned face and bear with him until he has told you his troubles and poured his tale of misery at your feet. My heart is broken, for false tales have been spread behind my back by a lady who once was my friend. She, with whom I exchanged sweet words and spent many tender moments, has spoken so ill of me that it seems as if all the women in this town join her in reviling my name for things I did not do.

O, mother, if you cannot stop their evil tongues, it seems that I must move to another land and start anew, for no woman will look upon me with favour here, and all of them believe the lies that have been told.

My son, I hear your mournful account of the scandal and slander that have wrongfully darkened your reputation among the women of this town.

In order to restore your dignity, you will take of the Oil of Mint and put into it Grains of Paradise, the bark of the Slippery Elm tree, whole Cloves, and Flax Seeds. And after it has mingled for three days, you will sprinkle it on your garments, so that it will act as a shield to your good name.

And you will put into your shoes the Powder of Attraction so that all women will be drawn to you and will not believe ill tales told about you and will rush to your defense. This powder you will put every morning in your shoe, one day in the right shoe, and the next day in the left shoe.

And you will make a novena of nine days with nine White Candles dipped in Mint Oil, with your name underneath the candles on parchment.

And in your pocket you will carry a piece of She Lodestone. You will put this in a bag of Chamois skin with the Magnetic Sand, and you will then tightly close it so that no one can look into it, and this bag you will carry in your left hand pocket and let no one put their hands on it.

But those who are leaders in speaking meanly of you, you will punish. You will take a bottle of Four Thieves Vinegar to which you have added Alum Powder and you will pass in front of their houses and pour some of this liquid on their front steps so that they will walk over it and step on it. And this is to make their tongues paralyzed when they speak badly of you.

Go you, my son, and do just as it is told so that you may enjoy peace and happiness for the rest of your life. So Be It.

38. THE LADY WHOSE MEN FRIENDS SPEAK BADLY OF HER

O dear mother, I come to you because of great vexation and a troubled mind. On every hand, I hear my men friends speak ugly words and tell mean stories of me, accusing me of unfaithfulness, double dealing, bad temper and flighty thoughts. They say that I cannot be trusted and that I love no one but myself. They accuse me of selfishness, untruthfulness, and dishonesty.

O good mother, they will drive me mad with their words of bitterness and scorn. No longer do my men friends meet me with a smile, but with their faces turned away they pass me. Seemingly I have no place to which I can go and be gladly received. My good words are met with contempt, my smiles are met with frowns. Can I hope for relief and help from you?

O my good daughter, the wisdom of the serpent, the peace of the dove, and the fascination of love will promote your peace of mind.

You will take of the Powder of the Wonder of the World, and on this you will drip the Oil of Confusion, so that the tongues of your enemies shall become as at the Tower of Babel when they speak of you and so that they will themselves help to undo the earlier work they have already done which has caused you suffering. And you will place a paper packet of this near to or in the house of every man who is your enemy, or in their shoes.

To the most guilty of your enemies you will write, commanding them to stop speaking ill of you and to desist in the underhand work against you. On this letter you will sprinkle the Water of Mars, called War Water, before you enclose it in the envelope. If they do not do as they are told, the Water of Mars is to bring misfortune and sickness to these men and put them in bad luck until such time as they make proper amends to you for their conduct.

To those men whom you wish to think well of you, whenever you meet them you shall put of the Essence of Musk in your palm, a few drops, so that when you bid them good day their hands will come in contact with yours and it will come to pass that friendship will become binding and strong.

In your house you will sprinkle Lovage on the floor in the four corners of each room and let it remain during the night so that peace will be with you. On your shrine you will put the picture of Mary Magdalene and before her you will say your prayers and you will ask her that your wishes be fulfilled.

Go in peace, my daughter, and do each of these things so that the tongue of the gossipers shall be stilled and paralyzed and their words shall be turned against them, and you will attain lasting happiness. So Be It.

39. THE MAN WHO HAS BEEN SLANDERED AMONG MEN

O good mother, I stand before you in distress, My name has been slandered, and the men who once enjoyed my company now only call upon me to share the bad words they have heard about me, hoping to see me flinch. My old friends are now gone from me. They pass my door and do not even look in. All those who were glad to bid me the time of day and eagerly take my advice when they were in need, now believe me not. When all of my friends are together, I am cast off and can find no place and no one to give my friendship to. Tell me, oh tell me, who has done this to me, and how may I find an end to this injustice?

My son, the man who slandered your name, the chief of your enemies, has long been jealous of your luck, and you already know his name.

Make an offering to the good spirits. You will take of the Red Brick Powder and make it into a wash, and put it on your door step so all can see. And when you go in and out of your house you and all those who are your friends will step over it, but your enemy will not enter.

And for the chief of your enemies, you will put on his front door steps of the Powder of Confusion mingled with crushed Poppy Seeds so that when he speaks ill of you, his words will not be clear and will not be understood, but will be confused and do him harm instead of you.

And if he continues in his blasphemies about you, you will take nine Black Candles, dip them in Vinegar and let them dry. Then you will anoint them with Confusion Oil and sprinkle them with Confusion Powder and burn them as a novena, one each night for nine nights, and under each one as they burn you will put his name so that the black wax will cover it as the candle burns. And this wax you will bury so that he too will be covered, buried, and forgotten and seen no more in his usual place.

And on your person you will put of the Essence of Vanilla, and of Cinnamon, and of Wintergreen, so that the thoughts of the good friends with whom your enemy had gossipped will again be for your good luck.

But in your mind you will have good thoughts for all of your former friends, and you will always go about with a kind word and a smile on your lips, even for the stranger. For you know not whom the stranger may be or where he is going, or even or where you will meet him again.

Fail not to do all of these things which are commanded so that peace will abide with you forever. So Be It.

40. THE LADY WHOSE LADY FRIENDS SPEAK MEANLY

O good mother, I am now before you that you may judge, for my lady friends have spoken my name from the house tops and from the hills, and they have attacked my character and questioned my virtue. They have said jealous things of me and caused my name to become a byword among the people. O good mother, I have to hang my head when I pass the friend or the stranger, for I know the viper tongue has reached them and that scandal and untruths have been called to their attention, and that they have heard dark stories and low sayings about me. Tears are in my eyes and my lips tremble. O mother, help your humble daughter.

Dear child, you who worship at the shrine, my aching heart and my pity are for you, so that I will again make the flush of pride brighten up your cheeks and laughter come into your eyes where there is now only tears. I will make it that you shall walk with your head unbowed, to look all in the face — and in order to accomplish this work, you will do as I now tell you.

For nine days, before you speak to any woman, you will chew a piece of Low or Little John Root, so that your words will sound true, and they will believe you and turn their minds towards you. These chewed roots you will spit around and about their houses before you speak to them.

And you will pour a few drops of Stop Gossip Oil in the water in which you bathe. And to obtain lasting peace you will burn a novena of one White Candle rubbed with Stop Gossip Oil every day for nine days. And in your home you will burn the Sandalwood Incense, and while the fumes are rising from it, you will stand in the center of the room looking towards the door, and evil will leave your house, just as the fumes are slowly vanishing, and leaving you clear. And in every corner of your house you shall sprinkle the Water of Peace until peace shall have settled upon you. This you will do for nine days without fail and with prayers on your lips.

And you will wear at your ankle the Japanese Tonka Lucky Bean. One of these you will put on your left ankle, attached and well tied with a thread of pure silk. And mark you well that you will not let a human hand touch this bean after once it has been on your body, and after you have made it fast to you. And when it falls from your ankle, its work is done.

Do these things faithfully so that the tongue of the viper shall be everlastingly stilled and so that the scandal and jealousies will die and leave in their place only great joy and happiness. So Be It.

41. THE LADY WHO CANNOT GET LADY FRIENDS

O good mother, an evil spirit seems to completely envelop me. I have no attraction, no sympathy from my own kind. My lady friends look an me with indifference. Their friendship is only lukewarm. Their interest in me has fled. I ask them and they promise, but they do not do as I ask. I invite them and they say yes but they do not come. They pass me by in the market place and bow to me sometimes, but more often they look me not in the face and pass me by in silence. They stop to speak to other ladies, but when I approach, there is no more to speak about and everything becomes quiet. I seem to have lost the power to hold my friendships with women. They look with the eyes and they see me not; they speak with the lips, but their words are empty and of no value.

O my daughter, you have truly lost your spirit, and for this reason your words to your friends do not ring true to them, and so they believe you not. You have lost your magnetism, and so you do not attract women to you. Look well to yourself first and then take heed that you value your friends.

For the spirits have said that she who wishes to get back her power to attract women must put around her neck a small bag made of the skin of the Chamois. And she must make the bag circular in form so that there shall be no beginning and no end to her friendship. And into this bag she shall put the Magic Sand and the Powder of the Violet leaf, which is shaped like a heart, and she shall receive the heart of the Earth, and the magic of the stars.

And she who would attract her own kind shall put on her body the Attraction Powder, so that the friendship she feels shall be felt by others.

And in the far corner of the drawer where her clothes are kept, a piece of the Queen Elizabeth Root shall be placed. And in her house there shall be cheerfulness and no evil thoughts, and she will keep cheer in her house by scrubbing the floor with clean water and Essence of Lavender flowers.

And in her bath she shall put a water brewed of Lavender and Verbena and drops of the water of perpetual youth called Florida Water, and a handful of the Salt of the Earth, that she will be welcome in company of her kind.

And to intercede for her at the throne, she shall have a picture of Saint Anthony of Padua in her house in the place wherein the company arrives so that they shall see the picture of the good saint and he will warm their hearts and their friendship for her will return as it was of old.

O daughter, do these things faithfully and depart in peace. So Be It.

42. THE LADY WHO CANNOT KEEP MEN FRIENDS

O good mother, I pray you to judge me and give me advice, for my men friends do not smile on me. They meet me and see me not. They forget me even as I pass. They do not remember my name. When I go to the feast I sit near the wall, unadorned and uncalled for. They have no bright sayings for me and care not to curry my favour, so I remain forlorn and forsaken while all about me is laughter and good fellowship. Lo, I am with them, but not of them. When I ask them to come to my house to visit me, neither do they say yes, nor do they say no. If they do come, they make no effort to entertain me, and they speak to me only in a cool and distant manner.

Dear daughter, I have heard your words of trouble and sympathize with you. In order that your bright star will shine again and that your mind will prevail, you will do the following things faithfully for nine days:

In your bath water for nine days you will pour ten drops of Special Oil No. 20. And in your house you will burn an incense made of Charcoal and the Blood of the Dragon. This you will burn every day for nine days in your house so that the smoke thereof shall penetrate the innermost corners of your house and drive away the spirit of evil that has caused your downfall.

And you will put on your shrine the picture of Jesus and before him you will burn every day for nine days one Pink Candle blessed with Sacred Heart Oil, and while it burns, you will stand in front of it and think of him whom you love, or, if you know not whom you love, then think of a man of the type you wish to love, and ask that he will make himself known to you.

And on your left leg you will put the garter of Saint Michæl, made of yellow and red. And affixed to this garter will be a red silken pouch in the shape of a heart. And in this heart you will tightly sew Magnetic Sand and the unburned Incense of the Blood of the Dove. This you will wear on your left leg at all times that you are away from your house, and let no human hand touch it after once you have it on your body, except your own. And on yourself and on your garter you will put Essence of Bend-Over and Oil of Roses. And this you will wear when on your way to visit men friends.

And, O my daughter, you will meet your men friends with a cheerful face and a smile, and they will say, "Lo, she is light of heart and must be wholesome; let us remain with her that our hearts will also be light and that we may be cheerful and in good spirit." So, my daughter, attain your wish and you will have many men friends and many beautiful presents. So Be It.

Conquering Bad Neighbours

43. TO MAKE THEM MOVE OUT OF THEIR HOUSE

O dear mother, I come to you to tell you of my grave troubles. There is a family living near to me who harbour wicked thoughts, and make trouble for everyone, so that there is strife and wailing wherever they may be. When I pass near their dwelling place they at once utter mean words, loud enough to reach my ears, in order that I may stop and say mean things in return, so that this will lead to a court scrape and the men of the law will interfere with me. When my loved ones or friends come to visit my home, they lay in wait until they come out and words of blasphemy and reproach reach their ears. An evil spirit makes them successful in their work of the Devil, but I hope to protect my home and my loved ones, and in the end attain peace of mind.

My dear son, I hear your prayer and will hasten to enlighten you so that all things you have asked me for and all things you wish for will come true.

It is the spirit of restless envy that urges your neighbours to bother you and speak words which may cause trouble and war, and if you wish to rid your neighbourhood of this spirit it is necessary that you proceed as follows:

You will take of the Hot Foot Powder and sprinkle it where your enemies will walk so that the fever to move will take hold of them and enter their bodies and they will become dissatisfied with their place of living and move away and not bother either you or your good neighbours any more.

And in your home wherein you abide, you will sprinkle Peaceful Home Powder all around so that the restless spirit who holds your enemy will not prevail against you and there shall be peace in and around you at all times.

And on your garments you will place a blessing that you will compound from the Oils of Cinnamon, Geranium, and Cedars of Lebanon mixed with pure Spirits of Wine. This you will put on the hem of your garments when you pass the home of those who wish to do you evil.

And in your home you will put the picture of the Sacred Heart of Jesus on an altar. And there, as a novena, you will burn White Candles of peace made of pure wax and anointed with House Blessing Oil, and you will burn one every day, for not less than nine days, nor more than nine days, even if your object has not been accomplished.

So now, my blessed one, go your way in peace. So Be It.

44. THE MAN WHO WANTS TO CONTROL EVIL NEIGHBOURS

O mother, the place where I have built a home for my family and children is beset by evil neighbours who create trouble for everyone. They own their home and cannot easily be dislodged. I have prayed for them to move, but still they stay, and because I am a peaceful person, I do not wish them harm. Please tell me, if it is possible, how I may rule and control them, since I cannot in good conscience destroy their lives.

My gentle child, your temperate spirit is admirable. For us to live joyous and contented lives we must be able to abide peacefully with others.

God does consider our relationships with our neighbours of utmost importance, for three of His Commandments concern our neighbours:

"Thou shalt not bear false witness against thy neighbour."

"Thou shalt not covet thy neighbour's wife."

"Thou shalt not covet they neighbour's goods."

If all people lived by the Ten Commandments and the Golden Rule, this could be a peaceful and happy place for all of us. Unfortunately, the Devil is hard at work, and our neighbours do not always follow God's commands. But although the Devil is loose in the world and he may work through an evil neighbour, yet there are ways to control the neighbour, and to bring peace and happiness to yourself, your family, and your neighbourhood.

First, give your house a good cleaning. Place half a cup of Reversing Bath Crystals in a pail of water and with it mop the floors and wipe around all of the doors and windows. As you do this, repeat, over and over, *"Turn back, Evil, away and back to whence you came."*

Write your name and the names of your family members on a paper and place it beneath a Block Buster Vigil Candle. Light some Jinks Killer Incense, make your wish aloud, light the candle, and recite Psalms 27. Let the candle burn straight through, and as it burns, prepare this mixture:

Into one pound of Epsom Salts, mix an ounce of Saltpeter, an ounce of Graveyard Dirt, an ounce of Red Brick Dust, and a handful of Rosemary leaves, as you make your wish for protection, rulership, and control over the evil neighbours, calling them by name. Keep this mixture in a sealed jar, and once a week use a handful as a yard sprinkle along the fence line or as a sidewalk wash, between their land and yours. They will come to respect you. So Be It.

Conquering Enemies

45. THE LADY WHO WISHES TO CROSS HER ENEMIES

O good mother, I come to you with my heart bowed down, for my enemies have sorely tried me, have caused my loved ones to leave me, have taken from me my worldly goods, have spoken meanly of me, and have caused my friends to lose their faith in me. On my knees I pray to you, O good mother, that you will cause confusion to reign in my enemies' houses, and that you will take their power from them and cause them to be unsuccessful.

O my daughter, I have heard your woes and your pains and tribulations, and in the depths of the wisdom of God, I will help your cause.

You shall take Four Thieves Vinegar, pour it into a shallow plate, and dip into it a sheet of parchment paper for each enemy, and when the paper has been well soaked, take it out and let it dry. And you will write upon each paper the name of one enemy with the Blood of the Bat, and send these papers to the houses of your enemies, tightly sealed with Black Wax.

But if you cannot send them, then you will hold each paper in the flame of a Black Candle rubbed with Black Arts Oil, until the paper turns to ash, then sprinkle the ashes, mixed with Damnation and Crossing Powders, before their houses after sundown, so that trouble shall be in their way.

Then, after a lapse of three days, you will take of the Water of Mars, called War Water, and in front of the houses of your enemies, you will sprinkle it after sundown. This you will do as you pass by.

And if it be a woman, you will take an egg, and with a needle put into one end Cayenne Powder and Goofer Dust, and in clear rain water you will boil it until it shall be hard, that there shall be no fruit from her womb.

And you shall burn a novena of nine Red Candles and nine Black Candles fixed with Black Arts Oil, one of each, every time the Sun sets in the West, for blood and for sickness, and let the waxes mix together all nine days. You will then take nine Pins and nine Needles, all new and never used, and boil them in Damnation Oil and War Water, and stick them in the mingled waxes, and throw them in drifting waters. You will do all of this to undo your enemies and take the power to harm you away from them.

O daughter, go in peace and do the work required so that you may have rest from your enemies and they will have no power over you. So Be It.

46. THE MAN WHO WISHES TO DRIVE HIS ENEMY INSANE

O dear mother, I have an enemy, well-known to me for many years, who persists in dragging after my wife, speaking ill of me at my job, and bringing misery to my home. I am a peaceful man, and will not fight my enemy, but I believe that his greatest weakness is an unsound mind and I wish to overturn his reason, so that confusion and insanity will be his lot. Dear mother, please teach me the way of the snake, for I am not a warrior.

O dear son, it is your right to avenge yourself on an enemy who has attempted to come between you and your wife, to block your money, or to destroy your happiness, but it may indeed be wisest to avoid a battle and work by stealth and subterfuge. Attend, therefore, to the way of subtlety:

At sunset, on a night when there will be no Moon, write your enemy's name nine times on a paper with Dove's Blood Ink to show your kind heart, and fold the paper three times. And when you have done that, anoint both your hands and the soles of your feet with Protection Oil, and place the folded paper in a small jar, to which you will add Black Snake Root, Vandal Root, Cayenne Peppers, Graveyard Dirt, and half an ounce of Double Cross Oil. Fill the jar with Vinegar. Make no delay, but on the same night, in the dark, throw the jar over your left shoulder into running water, calling out the enemy's name three times. Go home and do not look back.

And the next night, again anoint both your hands and the soles of your feet with Protection Oil, and prepare your room by touching Protection Oil to every door and window frame and covering or turning downward every mirror. Then, in the dark, rub a Black Candle with Jinx Oil and roll it in Cayenne Powder and Poppy Seeds for your enemy, with his name written three times and placed beneath it. Then wash your hands with Florida Water and prepare a White Candle dressed with Jinx Killer Oil for yourself, with your name written three times and placed beneath it. Light them both, and take care that you do not let them touch one another as they burn.

And when the candles are burned, bury the white wax and your name paper in your yard in a White Handkerchief that has been soaked in Florida Water and Protection Oil. But cover the black wax and your enemy's name with Confusion Oil and Restless Salts and wrap it in rough brown paper and throw it into mud or any filthy place far from your home, calling out the enemy's name three times. And leave it there and do not look back.

And pray for an end to your troubles and a beginning to his. So Be It.

47. TO CONQUER THOSE WHO HAVE MADE YOU SUFFER

O dear mother, I come to you with tears in my eyes and weak from the pains that I have suffered through the work of my enemies. The evil spell cast upon me by their ill intentions has caused me an untold amount of mental and material torture. They have kept me awake nights when I should have been asleep, they have tired me out when I should have been resting, they have made me worry when I should have been enjoying peace, they have made me cry when I should have been smiling, they have taken away from me everything on which I have depended for happiness.

O dear mother, I come to you to help me to reverse unto them the same evil spirit that they have cast upon me and to render them helpless to again hurt me or others who may have fallen victim to the evil spirit they command. I wish to make them suffer as they have made me suffer.

O my child, you come to me to help you in your hour of trouble. Although the spirit of revenge is not one to trifle with and is not pleasant to handle, I will help you only as a gesture of self-defense, that those who have cast upon you the spell of the evil one may receive the same agony that you have suffered and that it may serve as a lesson to them.

If your enemies are known to you and live in the same town, you will take the war-like Powder of Revenge and sprinkle it in front of the houses where they live so that they may step over it as they go in and out.

And you will burn one Black Candle anointed in Reversing Oil and rolled in Revenge Powder on their names for one hour every night.

And after three days you shall take the War Water and make a cross in front of the houses of your enemies and walk away without looking back.

In front of your own home you will bury one nail named for each enemy, pointed toward the street, but first dip each nail in Reversing Oil and sprinkle it with Confusion Powder that it may control the evil spirit who has been hounding you and send it back whence it came, to torment each of them.

Then you will scrub your floor with water in which you have added ten drops of the Van Van Oil and inside of your home you shall burn of the John the Conqueror Incense mixed with Helping Hand Incense and Spiritual Good Luck Incense every day.

Now go forth, my child, and do these things according to my instructions without fail, and you will get your satisfaction and you will be avenged, for the evil spirit will return to them who sent it. So Be It.

48. THE CURSE

The altar is set with a triangle of Black Candles that have been dressed in Vinegar and Damnation Powder. Write the name of the persons to be cursed on the candles with a needle. Place 15 cents upon the altar to pay the spirit. Place your hands flat upon the altar and say the following prayer.

O, great Lord, I have been sorely tried by my enemies and have been blasphemed and lied against. My good thoughts and my honest actions have been spoken of as bad actions and dishonest ideas. My home has been disrespected, my children have been cursed and ill treated. My dear ones have been backbitten and their virtue questioned. I beg that this, which I ask for my enemies, shall come to pass.

That the South Wind shall scorch their bodies and make them wither, and that it shall not be tempered to them. That the North Wind shall freeze their blood and numb their muscles, and that it shall not be tempered to them. That the West Wind shall blow away their life's breath and will not leave their hair grow, and that their nails shall fall off and their homes shall crumble. That the East Wind shall make their minds grow dark, their sight to fail, and their seed dry up so that they shall not multiply.

O Lord, I pray that their fathers and mothers from the furthest generation will not intercede for them before the great throne, and they shall become extinct. I pray that disease and death shall be forever with them and that their worldly goods shall not prosper, and that their crops shall not multiply. I pray that their house shall be un-roofed and that the rain, the thunder, and the lightning shall find the innermost recess of their home, and that the foundation shall crumble and the flood shall tear it asunder.

I pray that the Sun shall not shed its rays of prosperity on them, and that instead it shall burn them up and destroy them. I pray that the Moon shall not give them peace, but that instead it shall cause their minds to shrivel. I pray that their friends shall betray them and cause them loss of power and loss of their gold and silver, and that their enemies shall smite them both hip and thigh until they beg for mercy which will not be given them. I pray that their tongues shall forget how to speak in sweet words, and shall be paralyzed, and that all about them will be desolation, pestilence, and death.

O great Lord, I ask you for all these things because they have dragged me in the dust and destroyed my good name, have broken my heart, and caused me to regret the day that I was born. So Be It.

Breaking Crossed Conditions

49. THE LADY WHO WISHES TO BE UNCROSSED

Good mother, my house has been crossed and confusion reigns where there should be peace. Words of bitter regret are spoken where there should be words of praise, words of jealousy and doubt where there should be words of love, words of strife and crossed purposes where confidence or good will should be found. My dear ones look with suspicion on me and strangers hearken not to my voice, neither do they believe my words even when spoken with respect and truth. The stranger leaves my house in anger; my loved ones do not come to comfort me. I am desolate, uncared for, unloved, and miserable. O my good mother, I pray you to look with favour on your broken-spirited daughter and remove these crossed conditions.

O my daughter, when your house is crossed, it is decreed that you shall take of the Water of Peace and into it place pieces of the Root of King Solomon and keep it in your house for three days.

On the fourth day you shall sprinkle this prepared water in the four corners of your house so that no one will disturb it and no one will see it.

And on the fifth day, you shall burn the Incense of Solomon with Thirteen Herb Mix on Charcoal, with open windows, so that the smoke thereof will drive away the evil spirits and leave only the good spirits.

And on the sixth day, you shall sprinkle your house with the Essence of Saint Michæl, who drove the evil spirits away.

And on the seventh day you shall take the Oil of Van Van, made with the Root of Vetiver, and scrub the front door steps of your home as the Sun falls low in the heavens. And the evil spirits shall be conquered and shall remain away from your place and only the good spirits will remain.

Then you shall sprinkle your raiment with the Essence of Attraction, and when you meet your loved ones, friends, and relatives at the door, you will meet them with a clear face and honest words, and you will sympathize with them, and they will bring you cheer.

And in thanks for this, and as an offering, you shall burn a novena of nine Green Candles before a picture of Saint Expedite. Burn them all together, a little bit every night for nine nights, and you shall have great care that no ill wind will quench their flame. So Be It.

50. THE MAN WHO WISHES TO BE UNCROSSED

Good mother, my life has been crossed and my way is blocked. My friends, with whom I have always had peace, now speak badly of me to one another. My employer calls me to account for errors that are not mine and holds me back from advancement. My family is at crossed purposes when we should be in agreement, and much time is wasted in anger or in silence.

O my good mother, remove from me the conditions that were placed upon me by one who was driven by jealousy, envy, and disappointment to seek my ruin. I wish no ill on anyone, but only ask to live in peace and to once again enjoy friendship, love, and prosperity.

My child, if things do not seem to move in the direction you desire after many efforts to advance without result, no doubt there is a cross-force impeding your progress. This impediment can be best removed by getting at the root of the condition. You may suspect some one of holding you back intentionally or you may suspect some other psychic or spiritual phenomenon has brought about your downfall, but once the cause is determined, it can be dismissed and sent away.

If you know the name of your enemy, you shall write it on paper. If you do not know the name you shall write "My Enemy." And you shall dress the paper with Reversing Oil and burn it to ashes and then prepare a Double Action Black and White Jumbo Candle by dressing it with the Reversing Oil and rolling it in the ashes, and you shall burn it upside down, letting it stay alight for only one hour every day until it is consumed.

And you shall pour ten drops of Special Oil No. 20 in the water in which you bathe, and after the bath, you shall powder your chest and the soles of your feet with Uncrossing Powder, and anoint your garments and head with the Van Van Oil, every time you bathe, for one full week.

And after you have bathed, you will add to the water from your bath a few drops of Van Van Oil, and you will use use this bath water to clean your floors, the frames of your doors and windows, and the steps before your house. And burn in your house once each day, for this same full week, the Spiritualist Good Luck Incense.

And if, while you do these things, the one who put you under crossed conditions is revealed to you in a dream, or if his name is spoken to you, or if he confesses, boast not, but thank God, saying only, "He delivereth me from mine enemies," and go your way with luck and peace. So Be It.

51. THE WOMAN BESET BY EVIL SPIRITS

O good mother, the evil spirits seem to completely surround me.

During the hours when I should be enjoying happiness and have the mental comfort which rightfully belongs to me, I find that the pressure of the evil spirits is more than I can stand.

Day and night their shadows hang over me like a dark cloud that blocks the light, Everything that I undertake never materializes and the good fortune that was once mine has disappeared. No matter how hard I try to regain it there are always the same evil spirits blocking my progress. Every time I feel satisfied that I am about to receive and accomplish that which I desire, it seems that something gets in between and I can go no farther, finding myself in the same condition as at the beginning.

Therefore I come to you, dear mother, to help me to overcome the tremendous influence that those evil spirits exercise over me, that I may be happy, and contentment can once more be mine.

O my child, you come unto me in your hour of trouble that I may bless and assist you in acquiring the happiness and good fortune that was once yours, and which was taken away by the evil spirits called into your life by the jealousy and envy of those who have pretended to be your friends.

You will take the Get Away Powder and the Fiery Wall of Protection Powder, mix them together, and sprinkle them around the outside of your house at twelve o'clock midnight, for three consecutive nights. On· the third night you shall begin to burn three Reversible Black Over Red Jumbo Candles anointed with Saint Michæl Oil, and burn them upside down. This you will do for two hours every night, at any dark hour convenient for you.

In your pocket or purse, you will carry the Cat's Eye Shell wrapped in a paper upon which you have written Psalms 91 and 121. The eye will watch over you against the spirits that do the most damage during the dark hours.

After the period for burning the Reversible Black Over Red Jumbo Candles has expired, you should begin to burn your White Jumbo Candles dressed with Holy Oil, one at a time, for two hours every night, until you have burned three. This will strike the dreadful death blow to the haunting spirits. Release and let them go; do not converse with them as they leave.

My child, follow these instructions carefully and do everything that you are advised, and as the evil spirits depart, happiness and contentment shall be yours again. So Be It.

52. THE WOMAN CROSSED WITH SADNESS

O good mother, you see before you one who suffers from a frailty of spirit. While others around me rejoice in life, smiling and laughing at the many activities they undertake, and even rebounding from tragedy to seek joy again, I often find myself slipping into the shadows, enwrapped in sad and dreary thoughts. I am not ill; I have no enemies. I have groceries in the kitchen and my rent is all paid. Young men of good repute seek me out, but after even one night spent in my company, they ask why I am sad, and I do not know why. Truly, mother, it is a mystery to me, and I cannot see why I suffer in the midst of plenty. Please help me to understand this and to overcome it, for I wish to enjoy the happiness I see my friends partake of.

My daughter, your plight moves me greatly, for you are a young woman of bright prospects in whom an indwelling sense of sadness has grown, like a bitter weed which can not be easily uprooted. This soul-sickness is magnified by your sensitivity to the suffering of others. You cannot turn aside from them, nor can you help them, and thus you suffer distress.

Always remembering that the darkest hour is before the dawn, for nine days you will arise every morning before the Sun, and make a novena by lighting a Blue Candle for tranquility and an Orange Candle for optimism, and praying Psalms 23. Then, as the sunlight casts its blessings on the Earth, you will anoint the palms of your hands and the soles of your feet with the Oil of Crucible of Courage and, leaving your home, you will go out of doors and help one living thing. Be it a flower that you will water, or a poor woman whom you will feed, or a stray dog you will bring to shelter, each day you must lend your hands to aid another. You must act!

Consider this your sacrifice, and realize that a certain amount of sacrifice is important in your journey through life in order to attain the highest degree of happiness. By helping others, you will be better able to stand the pains and suffering of your own mind and body, and to finally control them.

When going out in the company of young men, dust on your body the Attraction Powder after bathing, anoint your head with Magnet Oil each time you dress your hair, and on your clothes spray Spikenard Perfume. Your companions will no longer ask why you are sad, but will see your inner beauty and feel only admiration for you.

Do these things in full faith, my child, and let the sunshine of happiness enter your life. So Be It.

True Messages from Dreams

53. THE SECRET OF DREAMING TRUE

My child, as a Spiritual Medium, it is your duty to develop a means of insight and a way to convey that insight to those who seek you out for help. In this book you will learn how to read the Zodiac and the cards. One more way is open for all true students of the mind: the way of prophetic gifts.

A reliable guide to divine revelations through dreams, as well as the influential prayers of the wise, is found in the Holy Scriptures of the Hebrews. There are diverse ways to gain such knowledge, but this will suffice to prepare you for the development of Spiritualistic control over your visions and dreams and to enable your interpretations of dreams, omens, and signs seen while sleeping and in daily life:

Begin with a short fast. Eat lightly in the morning, and do not dine that night. At sunset, pour a few drops of Dragon's Blood Oil into your bath water. Prayerfully dedicate yourself to the work, arise, and when dry, clothe yourself in white and cover your head. It is of paramount importance that you keep at hand the Spirit Guide Oil. With this you shall anoint your face, the palms of your hands, and the soles of your feet.

And after these preparations, you shall light a cross of seven White Candles anointed for mediumship, one with Holy Oil, three with Clarity Oil, and three with Psychic Vision Oil. And you shall burn on Charcoal the pure Frankincense, Myrrh, and Dragon's Blood Resins to empower your insight and remembrance. Sit thus in quiet meditation for one hour.

The dreams you have will be more clearly recalled and better understood if you prepare the Seal Number Seven of *"The Sixth and Seventh Books of Moses"* on genuine parchment paper with the pure Dove's Blood Ink. This is to be worn while in bed asleep. By means of this seal, you will learn through dreams and visions what you desire to know.

These steps, if undertaken but one time, will surely lead you to find further guidance as you develop your mediumship.

But now you ask, *"O good mother, what shall I do when I have a client before me in need of help and no time to sleep and dream on the problem?"*

My child, at any time, should you wish to consult the Holy Scriptures, you may take the Bible in hand, sincerely ask for knowledge, and the book will open to a passage that contains a key to your understanding. So Be It.

How to Work with Candles

CANDLE DEVOTIONS

Candles and lamps have been placed in this world to provide the faithful a means of showing devotion in a tangible manner. They have been employed for centuries in the administration of spiritual sacraments, and many hold them to be indispensable and state that every spiritual service, meditation, or veneration should be conducted with candle light.

The first Christians, being converts from Judaism, naturally appropriated to the service of their religion those Jewish symbols in which they believed. They used lamps in apostolic times, and under the Christian dispensation, when Bishops were received, the processions were led by candle bearers.

As a practitioner of the magical arts, your work with candles may begin with a prayer or with a statement of your desires, but among Spiritual Mediums, it is the custom that a prayer is said before each devotional candle as it burned and when it is first lighted. In these prayers you may ask what you want, and you should pray earnestly, with fervour and piety.

It is further recommended that if you are lighting religious candles to the saints, you begin with the following prayer:

May this offering, I pray Thee, O Lord, both loose the bonds of my sins, and win for me the gift of Thy blessed mercy.

After this you may address the specific saint with your petition.

It is very important that the candles will not be put out after each is lit, for if the candles blow out or go out, it is a sign of ill omen and the candle devotion should begin all over again as if you had started a new one.

An ancient custom holds that under each candle the wish that is asked for shall be written on paper or, in the case that you wish to influence some particular person, the name of that person is written on paper and put under each candle. The paper remains in place as the candle is consumed, in such a manner that the melting wax shall fall or be made to drip on the paper, and cover it as it burns.

Some Mediums place a photograph of the person they wish to influence under the candle instead of the name, and some combine the two, by writing the name and the person's birthdate on the photograph.

You have the power to determine what you shall create and when and where you wish to create it. Candles will aid you in your work.

CANDLES: TRINITY, STAR, CROSS, OCTAVE, AND NOVENA

The ancient religious custom of burning a number of candles according to a vow, or keeping lamps lit for a number of days has been handed down from generation to generation. It was practiced by the Egyptians and by the ancient Hebrews. It is known to the Chinese and the Brahmins.

- **A TRINITY OR TRIANGLE** consists of three candles. It may point upward, away from the supplicant, for aspiration, or downward, toward the supplicant, for material need. Salt or powders may outline the Triangle.
- **THE STAR** is made of two Trinities that interlock, balancing spiritual and material wishes. Salt or powders may outline the two Triangles.
- **THE CROSS** of seven candles is a vertical row of five candles for the upright and a cross-bar of two additional candles. One candle may be lit every day or night, or they may all be lit at once, as required.
- **AN OCTAVE** is a setting of eight candles, one each day for eight days or nights. It concludes on the same day of the week that it began. Among the Jews, a special helper light is used to set each of the candles alight.
- **A NOVENA** consists of nine candles lit on nine days or nights, one at a time. An old Church custom, it is also used in the home. It is not practiced by Christians of all denominations, but most will recognize it.

A lady can ask in a novena that her husband shall come back to her and allow all of his old loves to die in him, and that he will joyfully begin life all over again with her, and it is possible that this prayer shall be granted to her and she may be granted a better chance to live a happy life.

A man can ask that all of his old sins, mistakes, and debts of honour shall be forgiven him and make a novena on that, and he may have the right to begin all over again, in fact to make a new start, provided, of course, that he really takes his lesson to heart, and aspires to do better in the future.

A girl who has things she wishes to forget, or wishes another to forgive, or wishes to forgive in others, may ask by the aid of a novena that the sorrow of past painful events be wiped from the slate of her life, to be left behind for her benefit and peace of mind, and this may be granted to her.

A boy can ask for understanding in his studies and his duties, and by the aid of a novena it may be given to him that his old mistakes will be left behind and uncertainty will leave him, and he may make a grand success in his chosen field, where otherwise he might not have been able to do so.

OUTSTANDING SIGNIFICANCE OF CANDLES

Prosperity .... Yellow, Green
Love .... Pink, Red
Peace .... White, Blue
Attraction .... Yellow, Green
Dispelling .... Black
Revenge .... Black, Double Action Reversible Black
Work, Job, or Career .... Purple, Yellow
Harmony .... White, Pink
Protection .... Reversible Double Action
Holidays .... White, Yellow
Concentration .... Purple, White
Success .... Yellow, Purple, Green
Legal Cases .... Brown
Friendship .... White, Blue
Happiness .... Blue, Orange
Influence .... Brown, Pink
Bountiful Harvests .... Yellow, Green, Brown
Special Favours .... Brown
To Pray for the Sick .... White
To Commemorate a Death .... White, Black

Prayer Meetings, Circles, and Classes often use a cross of all seven candles of the spectrum at one time, consisting of Red, Orange, Yellow, Green, Blue, Purple, and Pink. If a special subject will be taught, then one candle colour may represent that teaching. No matter whether one colour or all seven are selected, two White Candles should also be lit.

In small groups, two White Candles will be sufficient, but no less than two candles made of pure wax should be burning during such services.

If commemorating a death, one White Candle and one Black Candle are chosen; the Black Candle to represent the death of the body, the White Candle to symbolize the life of the spirit.

For Readings or Special Spiritual Message Bearing Services, a Red Candle and a White Candle may be used.

Professors and Teachers of Spiritualism should keep by their sides the Holy Anointing Oil, with which they should anoint every disciple at the beginning of each class and every candle before it is lit.

BIRTH MONTH CANDLES

If you were born in January .... Red, Gold
If you were born in February .... Yellow, Blue
If you were born in March .... Blue, Green
If you were born in April .... Pink, Orange
If you were born in May .... Blue, Gold
If you were born in June .... Red, Blue
If you were born in July .... Red, Green
If you were born in August .... Pink, Orange
If you were born in September .... Orange, Gold
If you were born in October .... Pink, Gold
If you were born in November .... Yellow, Blue
If you were born in December .... Red, Orange

STAR-SIGN CANDLES

Aries Lucky Blessed Candles .... Red, Pink
Taurus Lucky Blessed Candles .... Brown, Pink, Gold
Gemini Lucky Blessed Candles .... Orange, Pink
Cancer Lucky Blessed Candles .... White, Pink
Leo Lucky Blessed Candles .... Yellow, Gold
Virgo Lucky Blessed Candles .... White, Pink, Orange
Libra Lucky Blessed Candles.. Green, Pink
Scorpio Lucky Blessed Candles .... Blue, Red
Sagittarius Lucky Blessed Candles .... Purple, Blue
Capricorn Lucky Blessed Candles .... Black, Brown
Aquarius Lucky Blessed Candles .... Purple, Black
Pisces Lucky Blessed Candles .... Blue, Pink

How to Read the Zodiac

Presented on the following pages are delineations or character readings which will apply to persons born under the twelve signs of the Zodiac. It will be found helpful to read not only the delineation relating to your own sign, but to read those of friends and family members. Included are the lucky numbers, gemstones, planetary rulers, days, and colours of the signs.

ARIES THE RAM

Born between March 21 and April 20

People of this sign know no fear or opposition, and swing through life overriding all obstacles. They are unequalled in earnestness and determination, and many of the world's greatest leaders were born in this sign. They are natural commanders, feel that they should be at the head of affairs, and usually dominate all about them. They have fiery tempers and usually do not work well under other people. They like to lay out their own work and do it in their own way, and should never be interfered with, lest they fly into a rage and abandon their undertakings. They are independent, have high and lofty ideas, and few things come up to their expectations. Original in thought and ideas, they are ambitious, energetic, reliable, and quite capable of rising to great heights in the world.

They have a keen sense of justice and when in a position of authority are generous, gentle, noble, kind, magnetic, and progressive. As a rule they are honest and square and will die fighting for a principle. They stay by their friends to the last. They love to entertain and are athletic and skilled at dance. They often appear to be wealthier than they really are, which may be accounted for by their commanding appearance. They may be extravagant in their dress, and are fond of nice clothes, as long as they are new.

Aries people are very good-natured and always ready to help those in distress. They are interested in politics, but are not the best of politicians on account of their fiery temper. They enter every battle to win, and never acknowledge defeat. But if they should lose, disappointment is very great.

It is hard to deceive an Aries person who has recognized his power of intuition. When they have developed the gifts of spirit, they will then grasp all. They should press onward, opening their soul to the eternal, and they will realize the great peace, happiness, and prosperity that belong to them.

Aries are most charming, handsome, and efficient, and would have the most beautiful temperament if it were not for their desire to lead the parade and their quick temper, which are the great stumbling blocks in their way. If they knew the great possibilities before them, they would learn self-control, and would school the mind to be the master.

Arians are ruled by the energetic planet Mars. Their Lucky Gems are Diamond and Bloodstone. Tuesday is their Power Day and Saturday their Lucky Day. Their Lucky Numbers are 8-41-62, 26-71-38, and 183-274-385.

TAURUS THE BULL

Born between April 20 and May 21

People born under this sign are remarkable in many respects. They are kind, gentle, often very generous, and overload themselves with the burdens of others. They are continually thinking about helping others, and often become miserable because they cannot help more than they do. Money to them is of value only for the good it will do, and because of a generous impulse they are often imposed upon by a tale of woe.

Taurus people have wonderful personalities. They are bright, witty, fond of dancing and music, and adapt themselves to all classes of society. They are magnetic and well-liked and take much pleasure in the friendships they form. They are close-mouthed, seldom talkative, but their mental powers lie deep, and people soon learn to rely upon their advice and encouragement.

The animal nature is strongly marked in Taurus people. They love nature and also love their own ease, pleasure, and comfort. They are very much set in their ways, and once their minds are made up, arguments and persuasions are useless. They will carry out their ideas regardless of consequences and they are often guided by a remarkable sense of intuition.

Undeveloped Taurus people are the most unreasonable on Earth. They demand their own way in the pursuit of their pleasures, and in their desire to possess things of beauty. Any opposition or resistance causes them to fly into an outburst of temper. They then wreak their anger on whatever may stand in their path, and the only thing to do is to get out of their way until their fury has spent itself and reason has returned.

People of this sign must be exceedingly careful not to be led astray by sympathy or flattery. They have the strongest passions of the twelve signs, and are overly lavish in their affections, with the result that a hasty marriage is often made early in life, which usually proves a failure. They have all the graces of Venus, and are surrounded with wonderful planetary and solar influences that render them open to all the new discoveries of progress.

They can command the powers of the universe if they would only raise to the higher plane of life and control their animal nature. Until this is done, much trouble comes to them and they may be disliked by those about them.

Taureans are ruled by the beautiful planet Venus. Their Lucky Gems are Coral and Emerald. Friday is their Power Day and Monday their Lucky Day. Their Lucky Numbers are 26-34-47, 39-56-78, and 917-826-735.

GEMINI THE TWINS

Born between May 21 and June 22

People born under this sign have remarkable intellects and are gifted in anything that calls for a quick, receptive mind. They can be extremely affectionate and generous. Courteous, considerate, kind, and gentle to all, they are charming, magnetic, and loveable, and have many friends.

A true Gemini is a remarkable individual, and some of the most wonderful people in the world were born in this sign. They are known for their double nature. They are happy and unhappy at the same time. They are in love and they are not in love. They want to travel and they want to stay at home. When they are married they want to be single, and when they are single they want to be married. They want to be rich and they want to be poor. In short, they are of a restless disposition and are forever changing from one place to another. When young they may be unreliable, and they remain young longer than people of the other signs.

Little selfishness or meanness is found among them. In fact, they are often too generous for their own good. They may make a lot of money, but they do not save it. They seldom worry about the future, and may meet with extreme poverty before they learn the value of money; then they will change overnight and become the most successful people in the world. As a rule they are not a success as wage earners. They belong in business for themselves, although as travelling salesmen or in some line of transportation where there is a continuous change through travel and meeting new people, they may remain a long time with one corporation.

They are lovers of books and read many stories, and perhaps cover a far wider range in their studies than any other people in the world. They are brilliant in conversation and can talk intelligently on almost any subject. They are often masters of many languages and are fond of tracing back into family history. Their marriages may take place on impulse.

Gemini being an air sign, they are fast, but they should always strive to associate with quiet, calm, thoughtful people, the determined and sure type of people. This will modify and bring more of a steadfast quality to the restless and changeable disposition of the Gemini subject.

Geminis are ruled by the swift planet Mercury. Their Lucky Gems are Agate and Chrysoprase. Wednesday is their Power Day and also their Lucky Day. Their Lucky Numbers are 38-56-23, 9-74-48, and 187-476-359.

CANCER THE CRAB

Born between June 22 and July 23

The Moon being the ruling planet of the Cancer sign, they are extremely sensitive, tender-hearted and sympathetic, and often generous. Their interest in public welfare is deep, and in some cases, when they cannot lend a helping hand, they become gloomy.

Cancer people are attractive, as they have most charming personalities. They are neat, and like to be looked up to. They display changeable attire and rearrange the furniture in the home. They are lovers of children and pets, and as this sign rules over the breast, they have a natural tendency to mother. However, they should not marry young in life, but should wait until they become more settled, for as a rule they are not satisfied with their youthful choices. When young, they often talk too much, and seldom keep a secret. If this habit is carried too far, they will have a hard time getting along in the world. They sometimes do not understand themselves until they reach maturity.

Arguments have not much effect with these people. Their feelings are too easily hurt, and they often abandon big undertakings because of slights or criticism. At times very strong and at other times very weak, they go to emotional extremes which cause their friends to marvel.

Education and culture are of untold advantage to Cancer people. They like learning new things, as well as changes of scene and occupation.

During the day these people are happy, while at night they may become blue, depressed, or sad. At such times, the world does not look very bright, and they are nervous and restless. It is then that they should seek some quiet spot and meditate on the higher things of life. This will bring calm and repose, and change the darkest and gloomiest nights to brightness.

Cancer people are natural born merchants and often successful manufacturers, well-adapted for active trade and business. They are excellent cooks and natural helpers, healers, nurses, and teachers. They are fond of the stock market and gambling, and have an inborn tendency toward the beautiful and artistic. Some excellent musicians, artists, and professional people are born in this sign, also lawyers and public speakers.

Cancerians are ruled by the fruitful Moon. Their Lucky Gems are the Moonstone and the Pearl. Monday is their Power day and Friday their Lucky Day. Their Lucky Numbers are 14-43-62, 27-39-58, and 638-917-425.

LEO THE LION

Born between July 23 and August 23

Leo people, owing to their natural goodness, create a happy future. When the true individuality of this sign holds full sway, they have high ideals, loyalty, and abundant love. They will give up all comfort to care for and nurse the sick. They are always ready to lend a helping hand. They never forget a favour, and never forget an injury. Some of the most emotional, loving people in all the world are found in Leo. There is a glow of sunshine that seems to linger about them.

Positive Leos are fearless and courageous. They often carry their plans to extremes regardless of consequence, but they have the power of mind to override all difficulties. Their courage and determination commands the highest respect and admiration. These people have a great love for children, and as to the management of their own are exceedingly wise, as they will not yield to the dictation of others.They are generally square and honest in all business dealings, and seldom, if ever, forsake a friend.

Undeveloped Leos are often impatient, hot-headed, easily angered, fiery, and passionate, and sometimes cunning and tricky. They are often chronic borrowers. The self-centeredness of this sign must be entirely overcome, and they should always have regard for the happiness of others, for only woe, misery, unhappiness, and discontent can come to a selfish Leo.

Much of their misery is brought on through their strong affection and passion for their romantic partners, and they often form their likes and dislikes at a glance. In most cases they are right. However, they will sometimes make mistakes that cause them sorrow, loss, and pain. Leo people should not allow themselves to become despondent or blue, for such a state of mind is very dangerous and may bring on serious illness.

When they wish to live a useful life, there are no better or more loyal people in all the signs, and no more magnetic or loveable people in the world. After Leo people have met great trouble, adversity, loss, and sickness, it is then that they will wake up and realize they must begin to think of higher and better things; and there is no limit to the great things in store for them when they once attain their higher nature.

Leos are ruled by the powerful Sun. Their Lucky Gems are Sardonyx, Amber, and Topaz. Sunday is their Power day and Tuesday their Lucky Day. Their Lucky Numbers are 30-43-56, 13-11-18, and 618-323-746.

VIRGO THE VIRGIN

Born between August 23 and September 23

Virgo people possess a great deal of magnetism, and among them are often found charismatic healers. They are generous and loyal. Naturally inclined toward precision, they excel at tasks that engage their intellects.

Virgos are very affectionate and devoted to their families. They have a propensity for making matches, being adroit at selecting companions for their children and friends, and for hiring workers for their employers. They enjoy companionship and are inherently affectionate, but it is hard for them to marry on account of their discriminating nature.

While at times lacking in courage and application, they aspire to become good and great people. Those of high intellect and culture can overcome all obstacles with grace and ease, and are often actively occupied in some elevating pursuit. The intellectually developed Virgo person fully realizes that lost moments and lost opportunities are sunken pearls.

Undeveloped Virgo people will seldom acknowledge or recognize their own faults, although they accurately see the faults in others. It appears at times that Virgo people are so busy that they have not a moment to examine themselves. However, the possibilities of Virgo people are very great when they once recognize that there is perfect unity in the universe, that the world is evolving, and that some good may be found in what seems to be all bad.

One of the faults of many Virgo people is their determination to rule and domineer other people about them. Because they are often more efficient than those who are not as adept as they are, they may interfere with other people's affairs, speak critically, or openly examine the faults of others. This tendency may make them unpopular, but, knowing they are right, they often will sacrifice public acclaim to do what they think to be best.

Virgo people as a rule are healthy, but if they imagine they are ill, they are apt to keep continually experimenting with drugs, medicines, and physicians. Many beautiful and charming people come out of this sign, and love and purity seem to linger about them. They love to learn, and they are admirably suited to a career in science or business, due to their capacity for organization and their understanding of technical procedures.

Virgos are ruled by quick-moving Mercury. Their Lucky Gems are Carnelian and Jade. Wednesday is their Power day and also their Lucky Day. Their Lucky Numbers are 72-14-44, 69-39-48, and 617-945-735.

LIBRA THE BALANCE

Born between September 23 and October 23

The people born under this sign are energetic, ambitious, generous, and inspired. They are of a jovial, happy disposition, fond of all places of amusement and they are popular with potential romantic partners. Graceful and neat, they dress well, but they are apt to be careless in money matters due to their love of sumptuous clothing, fine foods, beautiful furnishings, jewelry, and art.

In gratifying their appetites and desires they often become reckless, the same as they do when engaged in speculation. They seek pleasure and exciting sensations and new objects to interest them. Losses and disasters mean very little to them, as they are hopeful and strong and know how to quickly recover and get back on their feet again.

Libra people are generous to a fault, and will often give away all they possess to bring happiness to others, refusing to accept anything in return. They must learn to control this impulse lest it lead them into misery and grief by their bestowing too much on others. They do like their kind acts to be recognized by thanks or praise, but they may overcome this and do good deeds for their own sake and without thought of a reward.

Most Libra people have wonderful magnetic, hypnotic, and intuitive powers, but owing to their lack of faith or realization of the purer and higher realms of life, they don't know how to use them to advantage. When deciding important matters, they should always be alone, as they are more or less subject to the influence of those around them and often go astray when they seek too many opinions or follow the advice of others.

Libra people are quick and active in all their movements, and often impatient with the slow methods of others, which may lead them to sometimes become sarcastic and cutting. They do not get angry quickly, but when they do, they leave nothing unsaid and as it takes them a long time to recover from a bad spell of anger, they should be very careful to control their rage. When balanced, they are self-reliant, seek their own way, and find their own companions and occupations. They display much originality, and no people in the world have a keener sense of justice than Libras.

Libras are ruled by the lovely planet Venus. Their Lucky Gems are Opal and Coral. Friday is their Power Day and Thursday their Lucky day. Their Lucky Numbers are 11-27-48, 62-17-53, and 487-961-489.

SCORPIO THE SCORPION

Born between October 23 and November 22

The name Scorpio is ominous and suggests a fatal sting, but that by no means exhausts its meaning. As a scorpion or a snake, this is the most powerful of the twelve signs, watery and feminine, yet ruled by Mars; in all ancient symbolism the serpent symbolizes subtlety and physical power.

There are no more helpful people in all the world than the fully developed Scorpio people, and without them the world would not be in the position it is today, but would be in a rather sorry plight indeed.

If the people of this sign will cultivate their higher natures and train their naturally strong mental faculties, there is scarcely any undertaking in which they cannot achieve splendid success, and it is only the ignorant and violently inclined of this sign who fail. They are fond of good things in life, are usually neat and tidy about their person, and there is no more practical or sensible set of people in all the twelve signs than the educated Scorpio.

They are very independent and seldom seek help from anyone, and as a rule what they accomplish in the world is done through their own efforts. They are always busy and have no time to meddle with the business of others, and this is one reason why they are generally successful. Their love goes out only to the ones who are near to them.

Scorpio people are inclined to be secretive, and often their nearest friends are puzzled to know what they are going to do next. Some of them are very vulgar. Some of them have a low motive for every act they perform; they will use a friend for their personal gain and pleasure, and he will then be tossed away like an old garment. Yet should they later feel that they again require the service of their discarded friend, they will come to him as though nothing had happened, and gain his friendship back, as they possess much magnetic power.

Scorpio people are persistent and indefatigable in their efforts to carry out their purposes. Setbacks in life are not much to them. They keep all troubles to themselves, and with their great courage they go through life overriding all obstacles. They can be anything they choose to be, and can climb to the greatest of heights if they will but overcome their lower nature.

Scorpios are ruled by warlike Mars and dark Pluto. Their Lucky Gems are Beryl and Aquamarine. Tuesday is their Power Day and Saturday their Lucky Day. Their Lucky Numbers are 31-57-15, 42-61-70, and 561-269-482.

SAGITTARIUS THE ARCHER

Born between November 22 and December 22

The most noted characteristics of Sagittarius people are their great executive ability and their intensity of purpose. They are courageous, fearless, and daring. They know how and what to aim at, and as a rule hit the mark in all matters. They can see far ahead and can easily tell at the very inception how an enterprise is going to turn out. When they rely on their own judgement they are successful, but when they act upon advice from others they may make mistakes.

Sagittarius people, when in the employ of others, need but one telling. Tell them once and leave them alone, and they will carry out the most strenuous task. Lazy people are seldom found in this sign. Their health and happiness depend upon being kept busy. They are neat, orderly, and careful, but hey do not propose to keep grinding away all their lives at dull tasks. The talents of these people are many and varied. They can turn their hands to many things, will change careers or learn a new trade if necessary, and thus, as a rule, they can make money when others starve.

Sagittarius people are blunt and outspoken, and may make enemies by being so, but they feel that the truth and what is right hurt no one. One of the great faults of these people is that they expect too much of others born in less active or successful signs. They should learn to make allowance for people who are less gifted than themselves.

The people of this sign have a great love for children and animals, are kind, gentle, noble, generous, and wise. They are affectionate, but when their affection is misplaced, they often resolve to make the best of their bargains and to the outside world appear to be happy, even if miserable.

They despise all who are shiftless and lazy, but they have enough of their own manifold activities to interest them without bothering themselves discussing the affairs of others. They are honest, and never harbour ill will or bear malice, although they never forget an injury. Being naturally high-minded, they despise anything that is low and vulgar.

People born under this sign should be exceedingly careful in the selection of life mates, for a misstep here often means a misfortune in life.

Sagittarians are ruled by generous Jupiter. Their Lucky Gems are Pink or Yellow Topaz. Thursday is their Power Day and Monday their Lucky Day. Their Lucky Numbers are 15-77-62, 29-68-73, and 528-335-684.

CAPRICORN THE SEA-GOAT

Born between December 22 and January 20

The people of Capricorn are naturally inclined to study and deep thought, and many orators and teachers are to be found in this sign. Those who are educated have a persistent thirst for more education and knowledge, and will never rest as long as their intellectual attainments are not of the highest. They resent interference by those who tell them how to run their affairs, and they seldom meddle with the affairs of others. They hold that the secret to success is to attend strictly to their own business. It is best for them to be in business for themselves. They work hard and with pleasure in a team or on their own, but become miserable and restless when in the employ of others.

At times they are brilliant and lively. At times they become depressed, melancholy, and blue, and then they seek to be alone. They should get a good business education and learn to be self-maintaining and self-reliant.

Capricorn people are often indiscreet and eccentric in their charities and investments. At times they will give with a lavish hand and at other times they will not give at all, and this all depends on the mood they are in. Some of them are very proud, arrogant, and dictatorial. They are naturally independent and self-reliant, and are lovers of harmony and beauty. At times they are very high-spirited and all the world looks bright to them, and at other times they are depressed and gloomy and speak to no one.

Capricorn people are quick to know their friends, and can discriminate between flattery and sincerity. They are proud, abhor sycophancy, love order, and are easily confused when working under people who have no system, and they then may become stubborn and angry. It is sometimes very hard to get them to look beyond the external life and its daily tasks, but when they once become awakened and learn the spiritual truths, they become enthusiastic and faithful religious workers.

Constant in love, they do not display their affections and so may appear to be cool and calm, or even dignified and cold. Neither impulsive nor demonstrative, they are clean, neat, orderly, and systematic, and must be permitted to have their own way about the household. They possess rare ability in management, and many seek employment in the business world.

Capricorns are ruled by stern Saturn. Their Lucky Gems are Garnet, Black Onyx, and Jet. Saturday is their Power Day and Friday their Lucky Day. Their Lucky Numbers are 69-32-3, 13-44-7, and 732-417-576.

AQUARIUS THE WATER-BEARER

Born between January 20 and February 19

The people of Aquarius are among the strongest and the weakest in the world. They can rise to the highest heights or be utter failures. To what extent they may go lies within themselves, for they can make themselves what they wish. They are naturally endowed with great possibilities, and it is entirely their own fault if they don't succeed.

Aquarians have the faculty of learning things without much study. They seem to attract and observe information from every source. They seldom memorize anything, and it is not necessary for them to do so. They can always remember what they see, but sometimes forget what they hear. They will often earnestly seek advice from others, to which they then pay not the slightest attention.

Interested in the study of scientific principles, Aquarius people are known to develop or adopt the use of new mechanical inventions. They also possess unusual mental powers, but may neglect to use them. For those who develop their talents, however, the reward is great. Some of the finest spiritual healers that we have are born under this sign. Every Aquarius person is a natural healer, but very few of them are aware of it. They should realize that they really can amount to something and never sit about deploring their misfortune or inability to succeed.

Aquarians often talk about their affairs to others, and should be careful as to what others think about their actions. They must learn to bridle their tongues, and always remember that silence is golden. They should learn to be independent and self-reliant, ask favours of no one, stand on their own feet, and not lean on anyone. They should learn to use their own brains and develop confidence in their ability to succeed in any undertaking, and always press forward and onward until they have reached their goal.

People of this sign are as a rule pleasing and agreeable, with dignity on all occasions. They have easy, graceful manners, and are very loyal to their mates. They are quiet, calm, and peaceful people, with excellent control of their passions, seldom are ill-tempered, and make many friends. They may spend their entire lives in the service of others.

Aquarians are ruled by both Saturn and Uranus. Their Lucky Gems are Garnet and Zircon. Their Power Day is Saturday and Friday is their Lucky Day. Their Lucky Numbers are 12-37-14, 59-28-12, and 918-429-962.

PISCES THE FISHES

Born between February 19 and March 21

Pisces people are natural lovers, and their love is generally high and pure, and often goes out to the world at large. They are inherently honest, and seldom expect to see dishonesty or deceit in others. They are noble, generous, and wish to help all who are in need, and are often hurt through having too much faith in human nature. They are very loyal to their friends, can seldom see a flaw in them, and will stay by them through thick and thin.

Cultured, imaginative, artistic, and educated people of this sign readily discern the picturesque in everything. Being a psychic sign, they can sense the feelings of others, and they attract people to them. They often give away all they possess to help others, and then worry because they cannot help more. This is the power and force of their great love.

Pisceans are so sensitive that they become worried, despondent, and melancholy over trifles that never come to pass. They should overcome all worry and anxiety, and dwell more in the present and less in the future. They would do well to use more common sense and judgement.

Few egotists are found in this sign. They have little or nothing to say about their own abilities, and in many cases underestimate themselves. With their beautiful nature and the great artistic and psychic powers they possess, they should set about at once to overcome any feelings of timidity.

Pisces people are inclined to be careless, and will lose and misplace articles, sometimes due to nervous fear. They must learn the value of courage and confidence and perseverance before they can hope to rise to any great height. When they are in a bad mental state of mind, advice to them is useless, and they will listen to no one. The more they are talked to the more obstinately quiet they become, until they make themselves disagreeable to all with whom they come into contact.

When in good temper, they are kind-hearted and generous, and after they have overcome their desire to travel they become devoted family members. They are very charming and loveable, and are often found in positions of trust and great responsibility. Many people of this sign have lovely form, soft features, and beautiful eyes.

Pisceans are ruled by both Jupiter and Neptune. Their Lucky Gem is the Amethyst. Thursday is their Power Day and Monday their Lucky Day. Their Lucky Numbers are 29-73-48, 63-15-26, and 167-368-218.

Wedding Anniversary Secrets

HOW TO FIX PREPARED ANNIVERSARY GIFTS

The symbolism of Wedding Anniversaries may be brought into play by purchasing any pleasing article of the indicated material and dressing, dusting, or suffumigating it with Marriage Oil, Powder, or Incense.

At the end of the:

First Year	Cotton
Second Year	Paper
Third Year	Leather
Fifth Year	Wood
Seventh Year	Wool
Tenth Year	Tin
Twelfth Year	Silk, Fine Linen
Fifteenth Year	Crystal
Twentieth Year	China
Twenty-fifth Year	Silver
Thirtieth Year	Pearl
Fortieth Year	Ruby
Fiftieth Year	Gold
Seventy-fifth Year	Diamond

15. How to Read the Cards

THE SIGNIFICANCE OF THE CARDS

The following information is of deep interest to those attracted by the study of cartomancy or reading the cards:

The fifty-two cards in the pack correspond with the fifty-two weeks in the year. The thirteen cards in each suit symbolise the thirteen lunar months, and the thirteen weeks in each quarter. There are four suits, as there are four seasons in the year. There are twelve court cards in the pack, just as there are twelve calendar months and twelve signs of the Zodiac.

The following definitions of the meanings of the individual cards are based upon one of the oldest authorities dealing with the subject.

HEARTS

The suit of Hearts relates primarily to love, tender emotions, water, and family. It is roughly equivalent to the Cups suit in tarot.

- **Ace:** An important card whose meaning is affected by its environment. Among other Hearts it implies love, friendship, and affection; with Diamonds, money and news of distant friends; with Clubs, ambition and hope; among Spades, disagreements, misunderstandings, contention, or misfortune; individually, it stands for the house.
- **King:** A good hearted man, with strong affections, emotional, and given to rash judgements, possessing more zeal than discretion. A man with brown hair and blue eyes.
- **Queen:** A woman with brown hair and blue eyes or a fair woman, loving and loveable, domesticated, prudent, faithful, and loyal.
- **Jack:** A friend with good intentions, but not endowed with sexual desire. Sometimes taken as Cupid; also as the best friend of the inquirer, or as a fair person's thoughts. The cards on either side of the knave are indicative of the good or bad nature of its intentions.
- **Ten:** A sign of good fortune. It implies a good heart, happiness, and the prospect of a large family or at least a marriage. It contends against bad cards and confirms good ones in its vicinity.
- **Nine:** The wish card. It is the sign of riches, and of high social position accompanied by influence and esteem. It may be adversely affected when in the neighbourhood of bad cards.
- **Eight:** Affection. The pleasures of the table, convivial society. In association with court cards, it implies love and marriage.
- **Seven:** Friendship with a faithless, inconsistent friend who may prove an enemy.
- **Six:** A confiding nature, liberal, open-handed, and an easy prey for swindlers; when near face cards, courtship and a possible proposal.
- **Five:** Causeless jealousy in a person of weak, unsettled character.
- **Four:** One who has remained single until middle life due to being too hard to please.
- **Three:** A warning card as to the possible results of the inquirer's own want of prudence and tact.
- **Deuce:** Prosperity and success in a measure dependent on the surrounding cards; endearments, betrothals, and wedding bells.

CLUBS

The suit of Clubs relates primarily to business, travel, trade, and contracts. It is roughly equivalent to the Wands suit in tarot.

- **Ace:** Wealth, a peaceful home, industry, good health, and prosperity. A well-ordered life and legitimate hopes. Success in an ordinary career, or the attainment of celebrity in special cases. A rise in military rank or on stage, plentiful crops, a satisfactory business result from a journey.
- **King:** A man of medium complexion, upright high-minded; an excellent husband, faithful and true. If a letter arrives, it may contain a cheque or legal document. If the subject is ill, there will be a recovery.
- **Queen:** A woman of medium complexion, in middle life, with a trustful, affectionate disposition, with great charm for her romantic partners, but unsusceptible to attempted seductions.
- **Jack:** A business associate. A generous, trusty friend, who will take trouble on behalf of the inquirer. A business or contract lawyer, or a helpful doctor. It may also mean a dark man's thoughts.
- **Ten:** Riches suddenly acquired, likely through the death of a relation or friend. A long and difficult journey by water.
- **Nine:** Successful business. Friction through opposition to the wishes of friends, who may not fully reveal their thoughts.
- **Eight:** Love of money, and a passion for speculating. Pleasure in society. Good news will arrive regarding monetary matters or in relation to those who are away from home.
- **Seven:** Great happiness and good fortune. If troubles come they will be caused by one of the opposite gender to the inquirer. A business affair. A young woman capable of high devotion, even risking her life for another.
- **Six:** Success in business, both for self and children. A promotion in career or a victory in court.
- **Five:** An advantageous marriage in terms of finances, but fraught with disagreements at times.
- **Four:** A social gathering of some merit, but also a warning against falsehood and double-dealing.
- **Three:** Two or possibly three marriages, with money and travel.
- **Deuce:** A trusted friend. There is a need to avert disappointment and to avoid opposition when embarking on a journey.

DIAMONDS

The suit of Diamonds relates primarily to income, the financial aspects of marriage, and wealth. It is roughly equivalent to the Coins suit in tarot.

- **Ace:** A ring or paper money, a wedding or a betrothal, a present of jewelry, a lucky or talismanic charm.
- **King:** A fair man, but one with a potentially violent temper and a vindictive, obstinate turn of mind.
- **Queen:** A fair woman, given to flirtation, who is fond of beauty, society, and admiration.
- **Jack:** A friend or a near relative who puts his own interests first, is self-opinionated, easily offended, and not always quite straight. It may mean a fair person's thoughts. Money comes slowly.
- **Ten:** A wealthy marriage. Plenty of money, a husband or wife from the country, and several children and grandchildren. Ownership of property and the income derived therefrom.
- **Nine:** A rise in social position. This card is influenced by the one accompanying it; if the latter be a court card, the person referred to will have his capacities discounted by a restless, wandering disposition. It may imply a surprise connected with money. If in conjunction with the eight of Spades, it signifies crossed swords.
- **Eight:** Success with speculation. A marriage late in life, which will probably be somewhat checkered.
- **Seven:** A change in fortune. It can mean a good income, but with the need for careful action, or it may imply a decrease of prosperity. If accompanied by Spades, it signifies uncharitable tongues.
- **Six:** An early marriage and speedy widowhood. A warning with regard to a second marriage is also included.
- **Five:** In a general way it means unexpected news, or success in business enterprises. To young married people it portends good children. To those older, it signifies a longing for the past.
- **Four:** Breach of confidence. Troubles caused by inconstant friends who are vexatious and disagreeable.
- **Three:** Legal and domestic quarrels, with probable unhappiness and poverty caused by wife's or husband's temper or by interference.
- **Deuce:** An intriguing but not entirely satisfactory love affair, likely to awaken some opposition from relatives or friends.

SPADES

The suit of Spades relates primarily to conflicts, sorrow, loss, and difficulties. It is roughly equivalent to the Swords suit in tarot.

- **Ace:** It may concern love affairs, or convey a warning that troubles await the inquirer through bad speculations or ill-chosen friends. This is a directional card. When it is upright: A responsible position in the service of government. When inverted: Sorrow or death.
- **King:** A dark man. A man who is ambitious and successful in the higher walks of life.
- **Queen:** A dark woman, a single woman, or a widow. A woman of malicious or unscrupulous nature, fond of scandal and open to bribes.
- **Jack:** Personal thoughts. A well-meaning, inert person, unready in action although kindly in thought. A disorganized thinker.
- **Ten:** A journey by land, but also an evil omen, signifying betrayal, grief, or imprisonment. Has the power to detract from the good signified by any favourable cards near it.
- **Nine:** Illness or sorrow. An ill-fated card, meaning sickness, losses, troubles, and family dissensions. Nightmares and anxious dreams may bring more fear than is warranted by conditions.
- **Eight:** A loss. A warning with regard to any enterprise in hand. This card close to the inquirer means evil; also opposition from friends.
- **Seven:** A disagreement because someone who was trusted may not be trustworthy. Sorrow caused by the loss of a once-dear friend.
- **Six:** Hard work brings wealth and rest after toil. There may be a journey, unexpected or unwanted, but in the end it will prove to have been the right solution to a long-standing problem.
- **Five:** Bad temper, strife, and a tendency by an associate or rival to interfere in the life of inquirer, but happiness is to be found in the chosen wife or husband.
- **Four:** Illness, perhaps protracted or chronic, and the need for great attention to business or legacy if a death is expected.
- **Three:** A marriage that will be marred by the inconstancy of the inquirer's wife or husband, or by an ill-fated journey. Heartbreak, tears, and a likely end to a friendship, love affair, or marriage
- **Deuce:** A removal, or possibly a death that might have been prevented if only the warning signs had been heeded in time.

List of Supplies

1. ADVICE TO SPIRITUALISTS AND MEDIUMS: Power Oil, 2 White Candles, 2 Candle Holders, Holy Oil, 1 White Glass Candle, Peace Water, Master Key Oil, Jinx Killer Crystals.

2. HOW TO SPIRITUALLY DRESS HOMES AND CHURCHES: Rosemary Oil, 9 White Candles (1 for each room), 9 Candle Holders, War Water, Peace Water, John the Conqueror Incense, Master Key Powder, Glass Bottle, Laundry Sprinkler.

3. HELP FOR ONE WHO NEVER HAD SPIRITUAL HELP: Special Oil No. 20, Saint Cyprian Oil, Uncrossing Powder, Red Flannel Bag, Lodestone, Mojo Bean, Lucky Hand Root, Master Oil, Van Van Bath Crystals, Peace Water, Jinx Killer Bath Crystals, 1 White Candle, 1 Candle Holder.

4. A HAND FOR THE MAN OR WOMAN IN BAD LUCK: Red Flannel Bag, Lodestone Grit, John the Conqueror Root Chips, Adam and Eve Root or Pair of Balm of Gilead Buds, Devil's Shoe String Root, Holy Oil, Power Oil, John the Conqueror Incense, Good Luck Incense, Zodiac and Planetary Oils.

5. THE MAN WHOSE GAMBLING LUCK WAS CROSSED: Uncrossing Bath Crystals, Saltpeter, Protection Oil, 2 copies of the 14th Seal of Moses (Fifth Table of Saturn), 1 Glass Gambling Candle (Lucky Number, Lady Luck, Lucky Mojo, or Lucky 13), Your Zodiac Sign Candle, Protection Candle, Fast Luck Incense, John the Conqueror Root, Master Root, Wonder of the World Root, Chamois Bag, Master Oil.

6. THE LUCKY HAND: Red Flannel Bag, Nutmeg, Small Lodestone, Magnetic Sand, John the Conqueror Root, Wonder of the World Root, Wish Beans, Green Cat's Eye Shell, Frankincense Resin, Myrrh Resin, Master Key Oil, Fast Luck Oil.

7. THE GAMBLING HAND OF THE GODDESS OF CHANCE: Chamois Bag, Grains of Paradise, John the Conqueror Root, Lodestone Grit, Lucky Stone, Shark's Tooth, Has No Hanna Oil, Three Jacks and a King Oil, Mercury Incense, Good Luck Incense.

8. THE BEST GAMBLING HAND (CALLED THE TOBY): Nutmeg, Mercury Dime, Chamois Bag, Lodestone Grit, John the Conqueror Root, Devil's Shoe String Root, Five Finger Grass, 2 Lucky Stones, Jockey Club or Hoyt's Cologne.

9. THE MAN WHO WANTS TO FIND BURIED TREASURE: Wonder of the World Root, Lunar Caustic, Seal of Fortune of Moses, Dragon's Blood Ink, Chinese (Van Van) Oil, Cedar Oil.

10. THE HARD-WORKING MAN WHO WANTS LUCK: A One-Dollar Bill, an Envelope, Good Luck Powder.

11. THE MAN WHO WISHES TO GET A JOB: Crown of Success Oil, Lucky Hand Incense, John the Conqueror Incense, Chamois Bag, Lucky Hand Root, a Pair of Lucky Stones, Gravel Root Chips, Salt.

12. THE MAN WHO WANTS TO HOLD HIS JOB: Angelica Root, Grains of Paradise, Chamois Bag, Fast Luck Oil, Rosemary Oil, Crown of Success Oil.

13. THE MAN WHO WISHES TO OBTAIN A PROMOTION: Dragon's Blood Oil, Special Oil No. 20, Jinx Killer Powder, Algiers Powder, Crown of Success Oil or Attraction Oil, 18 Green Candles, 18 Pink Candles, 2 Candle Holders.

14. THE MAN WHO WANTS THE SECRET OF PROSPERITY: 1 Green Jumbo Candle, Prosperity Oil, King Solomon Wisdom Oil, Good Luck Incense, Lucky Hand Incense, Money Drawing Powder, Chinese Wash, Prosperity Oil, 8 Green Candles, 1 Candle Holder.

15. THE MAN WHO WISHES TO ATTRACT ATTENTION: Dragon's Blood Bath Crystals, Crucible of Courage Bath Crystals, Victory Bath Crystals, Crown of Success Oil, Look Me Over Oil, Magnet Oil, 3 White Candles, Double Luck Perfume, Hoyt's Cologne.

16. THE MAN WHO WISHES TO INFLUENCE PEOPLE: Special Oil No. 20, Influence Oil, Controlling Powder, Essence of Bend-Over Oil, John the Conqueror Incense, Helping Hand Incense, Master Oil, 52 White Candles, 1 Candle Holder.

17. THE MAN WHO CANNOT FACE HIS DEBTS: Essence of Bend-Over Oil, Yellow Dock, Sampson Snake Root, Jasmine Flowers, Mojo Bean, 9 Blue Candles, 1 Candle Holder Damnation Sachet Powder.

18. THE LADY WHO CANNOT FACE HER LANDLORD: Yellow Dock, Sampson Snake Root, Carnation Oil, Essence of Bend-Over Oil, 9 White Candles, 1 Candle Holder, Parchment Paper, Peaceful Home Oil.

19. THE MAN WHO HAS DIFFICULTIES ON THE JOB: 20 Yds. Silk Thread, Charcoal, Frankincense Resin, Myrrh Resin, Saint Joseph Chromo, Saint Joseph Beans, Rosemary Oil.

20. THE LADY WHO HAS AN EMPTY BOARDING HOUSE: Magnetic Sand, Fast Luck Oil, Saint Joseph Incense, Charcoal, Frankincense, Myrrh, Cedarwood, Sandalwood, Dragon's Blood Resin, Saint Christopher Chromo, Saint Raphæl Chromo, Saltpeter.

21. THE MAN WHOSE BUSINESS IS POOR: Jinx Killer Crystals, John the Conqueror Incense, Attraction Incense, Good Luck Incense, John the Conqueror Root, Lodestone Oil.

22. THE LADY WHO LOST HER BUSINESS: Magnetic Sand, Cinnamon Powder, Wonder of the World Root Powder, Mercury Dime, Powdered Blue Anil, Charcoal, Frankincense Resin, Myrrh Resin, Allspice Berries, Lavender Flowers, 2 Saint Anthony Chromos, Grains of Paradise.

23. THE MAN WHO CANNOT GET A SWEETHEART: Black Cat Oil, Peace Water, John the Conqueror Incense, Love Me Oil, Love Me Sachet, Hoyt's Cologne, Kiss Me Now! Sachet.

24. THE LADY WHO HAS A LOVE-RIVAL: Vinegar, Salt, Black Pepper, Whiskey, 1 Blue Candle, 1 Candle Holder, Guinea Grains, Cloves, Basil, 2 Apples, 2 Candies, Lodestone, 19 Red Candles, Saint Michæl Oil, Honey, Holy Water, Orange Water, Graveyard Dirt.

25. THE MAN WHO LOST HIS SWEETHEART: Special Oil No. 20, Attraction Oil, Attraction Powder, Return To Me Powder, 9 Pink Candles, 1 Candle Holder, Our Lady of the Sacred Heart Chromo, Love Me Powder.

26. THE LADY WHO LOST HER LOVER: Balm of Gilead Buds, Van Van Oil, Special Oil No. 20, Return To Me Sachet Powder, Chromo of the Virgin Mary, King Solomon Wisdom Incense, 9 Pink Candles, 1 Candle Holder, Parchment Paper.

27. THE MAN WHOSE WIFE LEFT HOME: Magnetic Sand, Rosemary Oil, Rose Oil, Lovage Oil, Reconciliation Oil, Essence of Bend-Over Oil, 9 Red Candles, 1 Candle Holder.

28. THE LADY WHOSE HUSBAND LEFT HOME: Horseshoe Magnet, Magnetic Sand, 9 Pink Candles, Saint Martha Garter, Return To Me Powder, 9 Green Candles, 2 Candle Holders.

29. THE MAN WHOSE CHILDREN DO NOT HELP HIM: Rattlesnake Root, Sassafras Oil, Saint Joseph Chromo, 12 Blue Candles, 1 candle Holder, Influence Oil, Influence Sachet Powder, Holy Water, Cedar Oil, Amber Oil, Devil's Incense.

30. THE WOMAN WHOSE CHILDREN ARE UNGRATEFUL: Chromo of Virgin Mary and Child, Frankincense Resin, Myrrh Resin, Charcoal, 12 Pink Candles, 1 Candle Holder, Queen Elizabeth Root, Geranium Oil, Rose Oil, Rosemary, Basil, Ivory Soap, Peace Water.

31. THE MAN WHO WANTS PEACE IN HIS HOME: Jinx Killer Salt, John the Conqueror and Lucky Hand Incense, Peace Water, Peaceful Home Powder, Essence of Bend-Over Oil, 3 White Candles, 1 Candle Holder, House Blessing Oil, Basil, Rosemary, Vanilla Sugar, Cinnamon Powder, Cloves Powder.

32. THE WOMAN WHOSE CHILDREN ARE IN TROUBLE: Bay Leaf, Wonder of the World Powder, Salt, Frankincense Resin, Myrrh Resin, Charcoal, Confusion Powder, Peace Water, 9 Black Candles, 1 Candle Holder, Black Pepper Powder.

33. THE COURT SCRAPE, OR THE LADY GOING TO TRIAL: Little John to Chew Root, Dragon's Blood Resin, Dove's Blood Oil, 9 Brown Candles, Victory Oil, 9 Black Candles, Destruction Oil, 2 Candle Holders, Wish Beans, Red Flannel Bag.

34. THE MAN WHO IS PURSUED BY THE LAW: John the Conqueror Root Chips, Black Snake Root Chips, White Handkerchief, Wintergreen Oil, Hot Foot Powder, 9 Black Candles, 1 Candle Holder, Holy Oil, Graveyard Dirt, Dove's Blood Ink, Parchment Paper.

35. THE LADY IN THE LAWSUIT: Goldenseal, Rose Geranium Sachet, Just Judge Chromo, Peace Water, Lamb of God Scapular, Little John to Chew Root, 9 Four-Inch Black Candles, 1 Candle Holder, Cayenne Powder, Poppy Seeds, 3 Six-Inch White Candles, 3 Candle Holders, Court Case Oil, King Solomon Wisdom Incense.

36. THE MAN WHOSE LODGE BROTHERS GAINSAY HIM: Controlling Powders, Goofer Dust, Cat's Eye Shell, Piece of Master Root, Psalms 133, Handkerchief, Rose Oil.

37. THE MAN WHOSE LADY FRIENDS SPEAK BADLY OF HIM: Mint Oil, Grains of Paradise, Slippery Elm, Cloves, Flax Seeds, Attraction Sachet, 9 White Candles, 1 Candle Holder, Parchment Paper, She-Lodestone, Chamois Bag, Magnetic Sand, Four Thieves Vinegar, Alum Powder.

38. THE LADY WHOSE MEN FRIENDS SPEAK BADLY OF HER: Wonder of the World Powder, Confusion Oil, War Water, Musk Oil, Lovage Root, Mary Magdalene Chromo.

39. THE MAN WHO HAS BEEN SLANDERED AMONG MEN: Red Brick Dust, Confusion Powder, Poppy Seeds, 9 black candles, 1 Candle Holder, Four Thieves Vinegar, Confusion Oil, Vanilla Oil, Cinnamon Oil, Wintergreen Oil.

40. THE LADY WHOSE LADY FRIENDS SPEAK MEANLY: Little John to Chew Root, Stop Gossip Oil, 9 White Candles, 1 Candle Holder, Sandalwood, Peace Water, Tonka Beans.

41. THE LADY WHO CANNOT GET LADY FRIENDS: Chamois Bag, Magnetic Sand, Violet Leaf Powder, Attraction Powder, Queen Elizabeth Root, Lavender Oil, Lavender Flowers, Verbena Herb, Florida Water, Salt, Saint Anthony Chromo.

42. THE LADY WHO CANNOT KEEP MEN FRIENDS: Special Oil No. 20, Charcoal, Dragon's Blood Resin Incense, Jesus Chromo, 9 Pink Candles, 1 Candle Holder, Sacred Heart of Jesus Oil. Saint Michæl Garter with a Red Heart Pouch, Magnetic Sand, Dove's Blood Incense, Essence of Bend-Over Oil, Rose Oil.

43. TO MAKE THEM MOVE OUT OF THEIR HOUSE: Hot Foot Powder, Peaceful Home Powder, Cinnamon Oil, Geranium Oil, Cedars of Lebanon Oil, Sacred Heart of Jesus Chromo, 9 White Candles, 1 Candle Holder, House Blessing Oil.

44. THE MAN WHO WANTS TO CONTROL EVIL NEIGHBOURS: Reversing Bath Crystals, Block Buster Glass Vigil Candle, Jinx Killer Incense, Epsom Salts, Saltpeter, Graveyard Dirt, Red Brick Dust, Rosemary Leaves.

45. THE LADY WHO WISHES TO CROSS HER ENEMIES: Four Thieves Vinegar, Paper, Bat's Blood Ink, 1 Black Candle, 1 Candle Holder, Black Arts Oil, Damnation Powders, Crossing Powders, War Water, Cayenne Powder, Goofer Dust, 9 Red Candles, 9 Black Candles, 2 Candle Holders, 9 Pins, 9 Needles, Damnation Oil.

46. THE MAN WHO WISHES TO DRIVE HIS ENEMY INSANE: Dove's Blood Ink, Protection Oil, Black Snake Root, Vandal Root, Cayenne Pepper, Graveyard Dirt, Double Cross Oil, Jinx Oil, Poppy Seed, Jinx Killer Oil, 1 Black Candle, 1 White Candle, 2 Candle Holders, Florida Water, White Handkerchief, Confusion Oil, Restless Crystals, Brown Paper.

47. TO CONQUER THOSE WHO HAVE MADE YOU SUFFER: Revenge Powder, 1 Black Candle, 1 Candle Holder, Reversing Oil, War Water, 9 Coffin Nails, Confusion Powder, Van Van Oil, John the Conqueror Incense, Lucky Hand Incense, Good Luck Incense.

48. THE CURSE: 3 Black Candles, 3 Candle Holders, Vinegar, Damnation Powder, Needle.

49. THE LADY WHO WISHES TO BE UNCROSSED: Peace Water, Solomon's Seal Root, King Solomon Wisdom Incense, 13 Herb Mix, Saint Michæl Oil, Van Van Oil, Attraction Oil, 9 Green Candles, 9 Candle Holders, Saint Expedite Chromo.

50. THE MAN WHO WISHES TO BE UNCROSSED: Reversing Oil, Double Action B&W Jumbo Candle, Special Oil No. 20, Uncrossing Powder, Van Van Oil, Good Luck Incense.

51. THE WOMAN BESET BY EVIL SPIRITS: Hot Foot Powder, Fiery Wall of Protection Powder, 3 Reversible Jumbos, Saint Michæl Oil, Cat's Eye Shell, 3 White Jumbos, Holy Oil.

52. THE WOMAN CROSSED WITH SADNESS: 9 Blue Candles, 9 Orange Candles, 2 Candle Holders, Crucible of Courage Oil, Attraction Powder, Magnet Oil, Spikenard Oil.

53. THE SECRET OF DREAMING TRUE: Dragon's Blood Oil, Spirit Guide Oil, 7 White Candles, 7 Candle Holders, Holy Oil, Clarity Oil, Psychic Vision Oil, Frankincense Resin, Myrrh Resin, Dragon's Blood Resin, Charcoal, Seal of Moses No. 7, Paper, Dove's Blood Ink.

We can make up any of these famous spells for you in "kit" form, with all of the ingredients and a copy of the instructions for use. Please see our list of prices at:
LuckyMojo.com/blackandwhitekits.html

Chronological Bibliography

Hartmann, Franz. *Magic White and Black or The Science of Finite and Infinite Life.* G. Redway, 1886. Uncredited source for *Black and White Magic.*

H. F. (A Fellow of the Universal Brotherhood) [pseud.]. *Astrology Made Easy or The Influence of the Stars and Planets Upon Human Life,* Wehman Bros., c. 1895. Uncredited source for *Zodiac.*

Foli, Prof. P. R. S. [Cyril A. Pearson] *Fortune-Telling by Cards.* C. Arthur Pearson, Ltd., 1903. Uncredited source for *Significance of Cards.*

Schertz, Helen Pitkin. *An Angel by Brevet: A Story of Modern New Orleans.* Lippincott, 1904.

Le Breton, Mrs. John [Cyril A. Pearson]. *The White-Magic Book.* C. A. Pearson Publishing, 1919. Uncredited source for *Spiritualism.* Reprinted by Red Wheel / Weiser, 2001.

Plough, Abe. *Black and White Almanac 1922.* Plough Laboratories, 1921. Uncredited source for *Wedding Anniversaries.*

Plough, Abe. *Genuine Black and White Good Luck and Dream Book,* The Black and White Company, c. 1925. Source for this book's cover.

Laveau, Marie, [George A. Thomas], *The Life and Works of Marie Laveau.* N.P. [Crackerjack Drugstore?], N.D., circa 1928. No copy found. Unknown page-count. Contents unknown. Presumed by Carolyn Long to be Hurston's source.

Hurston, Zora Neale. "Hoodoo in America," *The Journal of American Folk-Lore,* Vol. 44, No. 174, Oct.-Dec., 1931. 98 pages. Contains 30 *Consultations* and *Marie Laveau* (misspelled Leveau). No *Note, Spiritism, Candles, Cards, Zodiac, Wedding Anniversaries,* or *List of Supplies.*

Laveau, Marie [Anne Fleitman] *Old and New Black and White Magic: Marie Laveau.* Dorene Publishing, N.D., circa 1940. 68 pages. Contains 35 *Consultations, Note, Spiritism, Marie Laveau, Candles, Cards, Zodiac, Wedding Anniversaries.* No *List of Supplies.*

Laveau, Marie [Anne Fleitman] *Old and New Black and White Magic: Marie Laveau.* Fulton Religious Supply, N.D. c. 1965. 48 pages, abridged from the 1940 edition of *"Old and New,"* pagination in typewriter type. Contains 33 *Consultations, Spiritism, Marie Laveau, Candles, Zodiac.* No *Note, Cards, Wedding Anniversaries,* or *List of Supplies.*

Laveau, Marie [Larry B. Wright]. *Black and White Magic Attributed to Marie Laveau.* Published for the Trade [but rubber stamped on the title page Marlar Publishing], N.D., circa 1965. 40 pages. Contains 35 *Consultations, Note, Spiritism, Zodiac, Candle Novena, Candle Devotion, Cards, Marie Laveau,* and *List of Supplies.* No *Significance of Candles* or *Wedding Anniversaries.*

Allan Company. The *Guidebook to Black and White Magic: Book 1, Book 2, Book 3,* Richle Press, 1976. 16 pages each, for a total of 48 pages. Contains 21 *Set-Ups.* No other text.

Laveau, Marie [Dorothy Spencer]. *Revised Black and White Magic: Marie Laveau.* N.P., N.D, circa 1985. 64 pages. Contains 35 *Consultations, Note, Spiritism, Marie Laveau, Candle Novena, Significance of Candles, Candle Devotion, Cards, Zodiac,* and *Wedding Anniversaries.* No *List of Supplies.* This replaced the *"Attributed"* edition and was offered in catalogues as late as 1990.

Laveau, Marie [Dorothy Spencer]. *Original Black and White Magic: Marie Laveau.* International Imports, 1991. 70 pages. Reprints the 64 page circa 1985 *"Revised"* edition, with ads at end.

Laveau, Marie [Dorothy Spencer]. *Original Black and White Magic: Marie Laveau.* Indio Products, 2001. 66 pages. Reprints the 64 page unattributed circa 1985 *"Revised"* edition, with ads at end.

Long, Carolyn Morrow. *Spiritual Merchants,* University of Tennessee Press, 2001.

Laveau, Marie [Catherine Yronwode]. *Genuine Black and White Magic of Marie Laveau.* Lucky Mojo Curio Co, 2018. 96 pages. Contains 53 *Consultations, Note, Spiritism, Marie Laveau, Candles, Cards, Zodiac, Wedding Anniversaries,* and *List of Supplies.*